OPENING CREDI

Contributors this issue: Rachel Bellwoar, James Cadman, Jonathon Dabell, David Flack, John H. Foote, John Harrison, Bryan C. Kuriawa, James Lecky, Tom Lisanti, Stephen Mosley, Brian J. Robb, Allen Rubinstein, Peter Sawford, Ian Taylor, Dr Andrew C. Webber, Steven West. Caricature artwork by Aaron Stielstra.

All articles, photographs and specially produced artwork remain copyright their respective author/photographer/artist. Opinions expressed herein are those of the individual.

Design and Layout: Dawn Dabell
Copy Editor: Jonathon Dabell

Most images in this magazine come from the private collection of Dawn and Jonathon Dabell, or the writer of the corresponding article. Those which do not are made available in an effort to advance understanding of cultural issues pertaining to academic research. We believe this constitutes 'fair use' of any such copyrighted material as provided for in Section 107 of the US Copyright Law. In accordance with Title U.S.C Section 107, this magazine is sold to those who have expressed a prior interest in receiving the included information for research, academic and educational purposes.

Printed globally by Amazon KDP

A Word from the Editing Room

Salutations '70s movie lovers! It's here! Our magazine dedicated to one of the greatest decades of cinema reaches its seventh issue, and we're sure you'll enjoy what we have in store.

Allow us to begin by welcoming three new writers to our fold : Bryan C. Kuriawa, who takes a look at the much-maligned disaster film *Meteor* (1979); Stephen Mosley, who offers his thoughts on the cult favourite *The Rocky Horror Picture Show* (1975); and Tom Lisanti, who gives an in-depth analysis of the thriller *The Cat and the Canary* (1978). We're delighted to have them with us and we thank them for their excellent articles.

Many of the regular writers are back too. Rachel Bellwoar takes a look at the '70s movies of Maggie Smith; Ian Taylor gives a thorough run-down of the decade's 'Nature Strikes Back' pictures; Brian J. Robb tells the fascinating if doomed story of BBS and the Directors Company; James Cadman delves into the torturous thrills of *Marathon Man* (1976); and Peter Sawford assumes cover article duties with his an extensive look at the suspense thriller *Juggernaut* (1974). And there's more... much more.

It may seem like a long time since Issue 6. The reason for that is that in the interim we were busy launching an exciting new project. The first issue of 'Cinema of the '80s' was published in late August and has already attracted a sizable audience and widespread acclaim. If you missed its release and think it sounds like your kind of thing, it can be ordered through Amazon wherever you are in the world. We hope you'll head over and join our ever-growing readership.

In the meantime, let us tarry no more. It's time for you to leap into 'Cinema of the '70s' Issue 7. Happy reading! And we'll see you soon fo Issue 8!

Dawn and Jonathon Dabell

Remembering James Caan (1940-2022)

On July 6th, 2022, James Caan died from a heart attack and coronary artery disease at the age of 82. He'd been active and prominent in the acting profession from the '60s right up to his death (at the time of writing, his last film *Fast Charlie* is in post-production with an anticipated release date of March, 2023). The '70s boasted arguably his richest decade of screen work, containing many classic films and a number of unforgettable performances. He was Oscar-nominated for *The Godfather* (1972), Emmy-nominated for *Brian's Song* (1971) and Golden Globe-nominated for *The Godfather* (1972), *The Gambler* (1974) and *Funny Lady* (1975). His death marks the passing of a true screen legend, a bona fide icon of the film world. He is a star who will be sorely missed.

Caan's '70s film credits were:
Rabbit, Run (1970)
A Date with a Lonely Girl (1971)
Brian's Song (1971)
The Godfather (1972)
Slither (1973)
Cinderella Liberty (1973)
The Gambler (1974)
Freebie and the Bean (1974)
Gone with the West (1974)
Funny Lady (1975)
Rollerball (1975)
The Killer Elite (1975)
Silent Movie (1976)
Harry and Walter Go to New York (1976)
A Bridge Too Far (1977)
Another Man, Another Woman (1977)
Comes a Horseman (1978)
1941 (1979)
Chapter Two (1979)

Farewell, Mr Caan. Thanks for the magic and the memories.

3

In Memoriam

**Louise Fletcher
(1934-2022)**
Actress, known for *One Flew Over the Cuckoo's Nest* (1975) and *Exorcist II: The Heretic* (1977).

**Bo Hopkins
(1938-2022)**
Actor, known for *The Killer Elite* (1975) and *Midnight Express* (1978).

**L.Q. Jones
(1927-2022)**
Actor, known for *The Brotherhood of Satan* (1971) and *White Line Fever* (1975).

**Olivia Newton-John
(1948-2022)**
Actress, known for *Toomorrow* (1970) and *Grease* 1978).

**Nichelle Nichols
(1932-2022)**
Actress, known for *Truck Turner* (1974) and *Star Trek: The Motion Picture* (1979).

**Irene Papas
(1929-2022)**
Actress, known for *Don't Torture a Duckling* (1972) and *Moses the Lawgiver* (1974).

**Bob Rafelson
(1935-2022)**
Director, known for *Five Easy Pieces* (1970) and *The King of Marvin Gardens* (1972).

**Henry Silva
(1926-2022)**
Actor, known for *Love and Bullets* (1979) and *Thirst* (1979).

**John Steiner
(1941-2022)**
Actor, known for *Massacre in Rome* (1973) and *Caligula* (1979).

**David Warner
(1941-2022)**
Actor, known for *Straw Dogs* (1971) and *The Omen* (1976).

THE ROCKY HORROR PICTURE SHOW

by Stephen Mosley

The evening of Tuesday 19th June 1973 was a stormy one. As lightning flashed across the London sky, an equally storm-swept work debuted in the 63-seater auditorium above the Royal Court Theatre. *The Rocky Horror Show* was the creation of 31-year-old Richard O'Brien, a struggling actor, whose biggest claim to fame so far had been his stunt horseman duties in *Carry On Cowboy* (1965). Casting himself as hunchbacked handyman Riff Raff, O'Brien combined his love of rock 'n' roll and horror/sci-fi movies to tell the story of innocent couple Brad and Janet, who find themselves at the castle of cross-dressing mad scientist Dr Frank-N-Furter (Tim Curry) and his fellow aliens. On the night the protagonists arrive, Frank is unveiling his latest creation, a perfect specimen of manhood dubbed Rocky Horror…

In 1999, O'Brien told David Evans, co-author of 'Rocky Horror: From Concept to Cult', how his show, initially titled *They Came from Denton High*, originated: "I just wrote some songs that I liked. I wrote some gags that I liked. I put in some B-movie dialogue and situations. I was just having a ball." That sense of easy-going fun translated from the page to the stage, whilst also tapping into the emergence of androgynous rockers like David Bowie and Freddie Mercury - both of whom would eventually find themselves in the audience at the Royal Court.

Word of mouth soon brought other celebrities to the theatre, including Britt Ekland, whose then-boyfriend, the record producer Lou Adler, staged *Rocky Horror* at his West Hollywood Roxy Theatre. The success of this first American production led to 20th Century Fox greenlighting a film version. The studio gave the show's director Jim Sharman the option of crafting either a big budget musical starring Mick Jagger (with whom Sharman had worked as assistant director on *Ned Kelly*) or a relatively low budget ($1.4 million) equivalent with Tim Curry. Thankfully, the director chose the latter.

The only stipulation made by Fox was that two American actors be cast as Brad and Janet. Thus, Barry Bostwick (who originated the role of Danny Zuko in *Grease*) and Susan Sarandon (future star of *The Hunger*, *The Witches of Eastwick*, *Thelma & Louise*, etc.) received early lead roles.

Another American, a pre-*Bat Out of Hell* Meat Loaf, recreated his Roxy performance of ex-delivery boy Eddie, while the pivotal role of Rocky went to Peter Hinwood, a model who had previously appeared in Roddy McDowall's horror film *Tam Lin* (1970). (Shortly after filming *Rocky Horror*, Hinwood retired from acting and went into the antiques business. His singing voice in the movie was dubbed by singer Trevor White.)

It was felt, too, that a name actor should essay the narratorial role of the Criminologist. Although he was present on opening night and absolutely loved the show, Vincent Price turned the part down, as did Peter Cushing. (The era's third major horror star, Christopher Lee, would play the character on disc in 1995). The Criminologist's chair was, instead, filled by the icily suave villain of *The Devil Rides Out* (1968) and *Diamonds Are Forever* (1971), Charles Gray.

Jonathan Adams, who portrayed the narrator onstage, was cast as Dr Everett Scott and he was joined by his fellow London players O'Brien, Patricia Quinn (as Magenta, "a Domestic") and Little Nell Campbell (as Columbia, "a Groupie"). The latter part had been written specially for Nell after Sharman spotted her tap-dancing outside the Palace Theatre. Indeed, the now-classic song *Time Warp* was added to the show during rehearsals as a means to showcase the Australian performer's dancing skills. (The choreographer of *Time Warp* was David Toguri, who had staged the Satanic rituals for *The Devil Rides Out*.)

Also transferring from the play was musical arranger Richard Hartley (who reteamed with O'Brien for *The Return of Captain Invincible*, 1983); costume designer Sue Blane, whose anarchic style predated (and could be argued to have influenced) punk; and designer Brian Thomson - who had earlier collaborated with Sharman on *Shirley Thompson Versus the Aliens* (1972) in their native Australia.

Enlisted for cinematography duties was Peter Suschitzky, who would go on to light Ken Russell's *Lisztomania* (1975), *The Empire Strikes Back* (1980), Tim Burton's *Mars Attacks!* (1996) and several films for David Cronenberg, including *Dead Ringers* (1988), *Naked Lunch* (1991) and *Crash* (1996).

With cast and crew complete, the songs had to be recorded first so that they could be mimed for the cameras. The soundtrack was laid down over four days in October 1974 at Olympic Studios (the stage show band was fleshed out by members of Procol Harum). Reportedly, Susan Sarandon was terrified of singing, but she acquits herself beautifully on numbers like *Over at the Frankenstein Place* and *Touch-a, Touch-a, Touch-a, Touch Me*.

Although an equally nervous Fox threatened to pull the plug, production commenced on Monday 21st October 1974 for an eight-week shoot at Bray Studios - which, appropriately enough, had been the home of Hammer Films from 1951 to 1966. (*The Rocky Horror Show*'s original programme had contained a special dedication: "Special thanks to Hammer Films, without whom…")

Despite so many of the company's classic horror films being made at Bray, Brian Thomson told Scott Michaels, in 'Rocky Horror: From Concept to Cult', that he was disappointed to find that the Hammer props department was "nothing more than a shed", with little remaining

from their glorious past. Nevertheless, the tank in which Rocky comes to life is the same one used in Hammer's *The Revenge of Frankenstein* (1958) and, according to Bruce Hallenbeck in his book 'The Hammer Frankenstein', the bandaged dummy that lies in the tank is the very one that substituted for Christopher Lee's Creature in *The Curse of Frankenstein* (1957).

The 'Frankenstein Place' of *The Rocky Horror Picture Show* is Oakley Court, a reputedly haunted Victorian manor house situated a little further along the Thames from Bray. The building's forbidding exterior was familiar from such Hammer horrors as *The Curse of Frankenstein*, *The Brides of Dracula* (1960), *The Plague of the Zombies* (1966) and *The Reptile* (1966), while its interiors can be seen in *The Old Dark House* (1963). Although today a five-star hotel, back in 1974 Oakley Court was quite dilapidated. The *Rocky Horror* ensemble had to be very careful to avoid falling through holes in the floor. The uncomfortable shoot was further compounded by inclement weather. Sarandon even caught pneumonia towards the end of filming, but soldiered on regardless.

Diametrically opposed to such frigid conditions were performances that sparkled with vibrant sensuality and mirth. Chief among these is Tim Curry's dynamic turn as Frank-N-Furter. Curry's key into his character was the voice - inspired by overhearing two old ladies on a bus ("Tell me something, Deirdre, do you have a *hice* in *tine?*"). Once he'd donned stilettoes and makeup, Curry's transformation from shy actor to "sweet transvestite" was complete - the first of many powerhouse portrayals that

would go on to include Rooster in *Annie* (1982), Darkness in *Legend* (1985), Wadsworth in *Clue* (1985), the Grand Wizard in *The Worst Witch* (1986), the original Pennywise in *Stephen King's It* (1990), the Concierge of *Home Alone 2: Lost in New York* (1992) and Long John Silver in *Muppet Treasure Island* (1996).

Aside from the performances and songs, *The Rocky Horror Picture Show* remains enjoyable for its myriad, affectionate references to old movies. In the fantastic opening song *Science Fiction/Double Feature*, O'Brien's witty lyrics address such favourites as *The Invisible Man* (1933), *King Kong* (1933), *Flash Gordon* (1936), *The Day the Earth Stood Still* (1951), and *It Came from Outer Space* (1953) in the first two verses alone.

King Kong is also alluded to later when Rocky carries Frank up the RKO radio tower (permission for recreating the tower had to be obtained from Lucille Ball, who purchased RKO Studios in 1957). The Karloff-like pathos of this climactic moment is underlined when a ray gun-wielding Magenta emerges with a *Bride of Frankenstein* hairdo.

Another '30s classic, *The Wizard of Oz*, serves as inspiration both in the munchkin-like chorus of Transylvanians and in Sharman's unrealised intention to open the movie in black and white, then have it burst into colour with Frank's arrival. (There is a hidden option to view the film this way on the 25th anniversary DVD.)

Filming wrapped on Friday 13th December 1974, and once Graeme Clifford's creative editing was complete, the movie premiered at London's Rialto on Thursday 14th August 1975. Unfortunately, it was not well received. Christopher Biggins, who played one of the Transylvanians, remembered the premiere to Scott Michaels: "Everyone left the theatre wanting to slit their wrists. It was like coming out of a morgue."

Upon release, the movie drew terrible reviews and flopped badly. It wasn't until April 1976, when Greenwich Village's Waverley Theatre was looking for something to replace its midnight screenings of *Night of the Living Dead* that *The Rocky Horror Picture Show* finally took off. Within two years, the film was playing to packed audiences at over 200 cinemas across America, with some cinemagoers returning as a rite-of-passage. Among the Waverley patrons was a kindergarten teacher named Louis Farese, who, on viewing Susan Sarandon's rain-drenched Janet sheltering beneath a newspaper, yelled at the screen: "Buy an umbrella, ya cheap bitch!" The audience fell about laughing, and it wasn't long before more lines were added, props brought in and costumes worn. Thus was born the popular audience participation element of *Rocky Horror*, which exists to this day.

So, what is the film's lasting appeal? Why do its viewers become so obsessively absorbed in the action? For me, the attraction is in the unrepentant nature of the characters to be whoever they want to be, no matter how weird they are deemed by others. "Don't dream it, be it," as Frank so memorably croons. This is the whole ethos of the production. And this is why so many, including myself, find solace in this movie. After all, its creator could be considered an outsider himself.

There's a lyric in the song *Don't Dream It* where Frank admits to crying at the sight of Fay Wray's "satin-draped frame", presumably on a childhood viewing of *King Kong*, "because I wanted to be dressed just the same." Although the line always gets a laugh whenever I've seen the film in company, I've always detected a real sense of pain behind this lyric. My suspicion was confirmed on viewing *An Evening with Richard O'Brien* (2008), wherein O'Brien tells interviewer Mark Salisbury: "I am transgendered. I wouldn't wish it on anybody, it's a difficult journey... I knew at the age of six that I wanted to be a girl." Unable to express these feelings when young, especially in a "misogynistic society", O'Brien took to "living inside his head." The dreams and ideas that O'Brien locked away were given free rein in *Rocky Horror*, the eventual esteem of which played some part in allowing a progressively permissive society to grow more understanding still. As O'Brien told VH1's *Behind the Music*: "If I have in any way enabled people who felt lost and uncomfortable about their nature to live in a happier world, [then] thank God I did something worthwhile on the planet."

Stephen Mosley is the author of 'Christopher Lee: The Loneliness of Evil' (Midnight Marquee Press).

HIGH VELOCITY

by Jonathon Dabell

High Velocity (1976) was supposed to mark the start of a lucrative series of American films shot in the Philippines. Filmways were key players in the project; their idea was to employ American stars alongside Filipino supporting actors and crew members - and to utilise Filipino resources and facilities - with the aim of releasing, distributing and promoting movies through a production company called First Asian Films of California. Alas, *High Velocity* was the only film to be completed by First Asian. Soon after, the company vanished from the cinematic landscape quicker than it had appeared. Its second film would have been a proposed $4-million epic about the life and career of famed American officer John J. Pershing, but it never got beyond development stage.

First-time producer Takafumi Ohashi hired the inexperienced Remi Kramer to direct this flagship production which, for a time, was the most expensive film made in the Philippines. Kramer had previously designed the titles for *The Doris Day Show* (1968-1973) as well as directing several Marlboro Man commercials. He'd also won a Clio award for his work in television advertising. It was a gamble on Ohashi's part to entrust the reins to someone whose background was in commercials and designing titles for TV shows. The gamble didn't fail but it didn't exactly pay off either - *High Velocity*, while solid, gritty and interesting, did nothing at the box office and would prove Kramer's only feature-length directorial gig.

Some relatively big names were brought in to work behind the scenes. The cinematography fell to the experienced Robert Paynter, whose credits included the likes of *Hannibal Brooks* (1969), *Chato's Land* (1972) and *Scorpio* (1973) for Michael Winner (later he'd work with Richard Donner on *Superman II* and John Landis on *An American Werewolf in London*). Legendary composer Jerry Goldsmith was hired to do the score. Editor David Bretherton could boast such classics as *The Train* (1964), *Save the Tiger* (1973) and *Westworld* (1973) on his resumé. More impressively, he'd picked up an Oscar for his work on *Cabaret* (1972).

There were big, familiar faces in front of the camera too. Ben Gazzara had carved himself a tidy career by flitting between major Hollywood productions, TV shows and Italian crime thrillers. He'd also recently become a favourite character-actor of indie filmmaker (and oftentimes actor) John Cassavetes. In fact, *High Velocity* was released shortly after Gazzara had appeared in one of his most celebrated roles as Cosmo Vittelli in Cassavetes' *The Killing of a Chinese Bookie*. Then there was Britt Ekland, a Swedish-born sex symbol who'd been married to Peter Sellers and appeared in high-profile films like *The Wicker Man* (1973) and *The Man with the Golden Gun* (1974). Paul Winfield was one of the rising black stars of the period, his filmography boasting several notable blaxploitation hits as well as eclectic fare in a variety of other genres. Rounding off the main quartet was Keenan Wynn, a familiar supporting player who had (and would continue to) appear in everything from bona fide classics to the most unmentionable drivel. Argentinian actor Alejandro Rey and the recognisable Victoria Racimo were also cast in substantial roles.

High Velocity would seem at first glance to be a standard mercenary adventure flick, worthy of being classified in the same bracket as *Dark of the Sun* (1968), *The Wild Geese* (1978) and *The Dogs of War* (1980). However, it doesn't quite sit right amid such company because its moral standpoint is somewhat muddier.

Within the first ten minutes, we witness the abduction

HAUTE TENSION

HAUTE TENSION

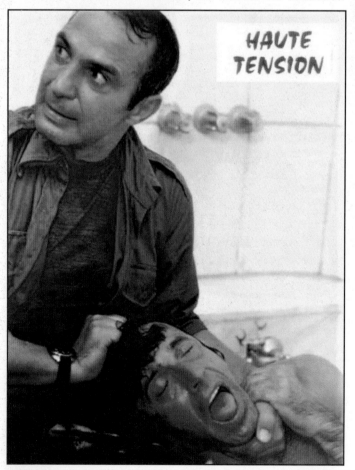

HAUTE TENSION

of William Anderson (Wynn), the Far East director of the Global Satellite Corporation, a fictitious greedy international business consortium which has been raping and exploiting the resources of an unnamed banana republic in SE Asia. From the very first scene, we see and hear Anderson acting like a complete asshole towards his staff and the local population. He isn't particularly pleasant to his 'trophy' wife Marie (Ekland) either. When we first meet him, he's barking insults and instructions at some poor subordinate down a telephone line. His kidnapping occurs at a local polo club, where impoverished locals stare miserably through barred iron gates while rich foreigners and corrupt nationals indulge themselves with expensive food and drink and modern comforts. Even the polo players are privileged jerks (one breaks his mallet, and takes out his frustrations by beating an innocent equipment boy with it). This opening ten-minute sequence quickly establishes that Anderson is an awful human being - the company he works for, the club he frequents, the people he mixes with are equally rotten. As Jerry Goldsmith's thunderous score brings the opening sequence to a close, we get the sense that we're supposed to be on the side of the kidnappers, a guerrilla group who call themselves the 'Gang of 45'. They certainly seem justified in nabbing this odious, obnoxious American capitalist. Our expectation is that the rest of the story will depict them making him pay for his actions against their country.

But things take an unexpected turn. Anderson's right-hand man, Martel (Rey), hires a couple of ex-Vietnam vets who now live in the country to get Anderson back. One is Cliff Baumgartner (Gazzara) who has married a local girl and tried to escape his violent past by starting a crop-dusting business. The other is Willy Watson (Winfield) who spends most of his days boozing, gambling and whoring. He's lost his way and craves a return to the sense of purpose, action and danger he felt during his military days. Baumgartner is reluctant about the job but knows his wife will be victimised if he refuses. He is also tantalised by the $100,000 reward for completing the operation. Watson, however, is thrilled to be back in his army camouflages, armed to the teeth with an objective to fulfil.

"You love it, don't you?" remarks Baumgartner.

"And I suppose you don't, huh?" Watson retorts sardonically.

"Yeah," confesses Baumgartner. "But I don't *like* lovin' it."

We quickly come to favour Baumgartner and Watson. They have real rapport and chemistry, and throw themselves into various scrapes with aplomb. Their love of adventure is infectious. Their mutual respect is palpable. If I was in the army, they're the kind of guys I'd want in my platoon. What we don't recognise straight away, or what we overlook due to their affableness, is that they're actually pretty bad guys who have been hired by a rotten corporation to rescue a horrible man. We don't realise right away that we've been steered into rooting for the 'bad' team. By the time we remember Gazzara and Winfield are technically bad guys, we've grown to like them too much to want them to fail.

As the story progresses, the pair gleefully unleash an array of weapons against the guerrillas who have kidnapped Wynn. It's only when we remember that Anderson is not worth saving, that our trigger-happy anti-heroes are attempting to liberate a tyrant, that we sense the story is heading for grim, nihilistic territory.

Indeed, by the end there have been enough killings, betrayals and twists to leave a sour taste in anyone's mouth. There are no winners here, except maybe the barely-seen corrupt capitalists. Everyone is either dead or scarred by their involvement in the events. There's an ugly, cynical tone throughout. We feel sorry on one hand for the 'Gang of 45' when their stronghold is destroyed and with it the tapes on which they have gathered evidence against Anderson and his corporation. Yet on the other hand, we feel equally bitter about the fate of Baumgartner and Watson whose very actions caused the death of the guerrillas and ruined their evidence. That's the muddy moral standpoint I mentioned earlier. We find

ourselves invested in completely opposite sides - we want Baumgartner and Watson to succeed and survive, yet we want the guerrillas to get information out of Anderson and then kill the cantankerous old son-of-a-bitch. It's that paradox which makes *High Velocity* interesting and gives it a fresh dimension from the usual mercenary adventure schtick.

There are drawbacks, yes, one being the slightly too-dim photography (a pretty good chase sequence is held back from being excellent by being too dark to see properly), another being the fact that the 'Corporation' is under-developed and we're never quite sure why we're supposed to view them as such evil people. But there's good stuff here, especially Gazzara as the lead (who better than him to portray a simmering soldier of fortune, charming one moment, raging the next?) and Jerry Goldsmith's score, which really adds to the sweaty jungle atmosphere.

High Velocity is a solid film, too long ignored. It's criminal that it's only available on grainy VHS, off-air TV recordings or dubious quality DVD-R bootlegs. It deserves a cleaned-up DVD or Blu-ray release so that people can see it as it was meant to be seen. Fans of offbeat action pics and cynical political/military dramas will find it worth a look.

TRAVELS WITH MAGGIE SMITH:
An Overview of Her '70s Film Work

by Rachel Bellwoar

Coming off her first Oscar win for *The Prime of Miss Jean Brodie* (1969), the '70s would see Maggie Smith devote much of her time to the theater, accumulating two Tony nominations in the process for Noël Coward's *Private Lives* (1975) and Tom Stoppard's *Night and Day* (1979) (though the latter nomination would come in 1980). That Smith found time to be in five films during the decade was surely helped by the fact that three of them involved large ensemble casts - the kind of star-studded pictures where the opening credits are a joy, because as each heavy-hitting name appears you think it's going to be impossible to top, then the next big name pops up and proves you wrong.

Smith's first film of the decade wasn't one of those. In a scene that feels reminiscent of *Harold and Maude* (1971) (though Graham Greene's source novel predates it by two years), George Cukor's *Travels with My Aunt* (1972) begins with Augusta (Smith) and Henry (Alec McCowen) meeting at a funeral. Unlike Harold and Maude, they're not funeral crashers and they're not destined to be lovers. Henry might not recognize her (he was told she was dead), but Augusta is his aunt, and the deceased woman Angelica was her sister. She wasn't, however, Henry's mother. Augusta drops this bombshell by telling Henry her sister should've had a white funeral.

For her part, Augusta is dressed in black and, like many of the costumes designed for Smith by Anthony Powell in this movie (they would work together again in the '70s on *Death on the Nile*), it's a very ostentatious and skin-covering look (all the better to hide the fact that Smith is much younger than the older woman she's supposed to be playing). Making her look older is the name of the game in terms of José Antonio

Sánchez's make-up as well, which adds wrinkles to her face and gives her an almost sheet-white complexion, all the more garish when contrasted with Augusta's lavender eye shadow and red lipstick. That this is intentional is confirmed in the flashbacks, where Augusta is younger and in love with Mr. Visconti (played by Smith's then-husband Robert Stephens). Then Smith is allowed to look more natural, but Augusta is an eccentric character (the cliched "fun aunt") and her clothes and appearance reflect that.

It's in the contrast between Augusta's appearance and her agility that Smith gets the most laughs. Augusta didn't seek out her nephew just to pay her respects (and, while it's not the first time Augusta's ulterior motives are hinted at, Augusta comes closest to giving herself away when she interrupts him to ask: "Are you still at the bank, Henry?" when he's in the middle of telling her about Angelica's final days). It turns out Mr. Visconti is being held for ransom and the film's title is a reference to Henry getting roped into helping Augusta raise enough funds to free him from his captors.

For all the emphasis on Augusta being past her prime (the opposite of Miss Jean Brodie), Smith doesn't play her as an old woman. That isn't to say that women past a certain age are without energy or that all adults face the same mobility issues, but there's being able to walk and there's throwing yourself onto a bed with abandon. Augusta never takes any precautions.

Mr. Visconti's ear arrives in the mail and while the shot is framed in such a way that's it's possible Smith doesn't

fall to the ground or that there is something there to soften the blow, the idea is that Augusta has fainted and yet suffers no injury. No broken hip, nothing.

Rather than these moments sticking out as being unrealistic (which they technically are), they only work to make Augusta (and Smith) more endearing. While the film loses momentum over the course of its runtime (instead of being used to further Augusta's character, the before-mentioned flashbacks are pure bloat), none of that is Smith's fault. She earned her second Oscar nomination as Best Actress for the role but lost to Liza Minnelli in *Cabaret*.

A role that doesn't get its due is her performance as Lila Fisher in Alan J. Pakula's *Love and Pain and the Whole Damn Thing* (1973). For those who only know Pakula for his paranoia trilogy (*Klute*, *All the President's Men* and *The Parallax View*), *Love and Pain and the Whole Damn Thing* is a different animal, but one buoyed by two guileless performances courtesy of Smith and Timothy Bottoms (as Walter Elbertson) and a screenplay by Alvin Sargent (*Ordinary People*, *Paper Moon*).

Plagued by insecurities made worse by his demanding and academically gifted parents, Walter is fine not having plans for the summer until his family sign him up for a bike tour of Spain. Unable to keep up with the other bikers

or retain any of the Spanish his tour guide Carl (Lloyd Brimhall) tries to teach him, Walter hears English at the next table and jumps at the chance to join a bus tour of Spain instead (one benefit of having scholarly parents is that money is no object for him).

In *The Graduate* (1967), Dustin Hoffman and Katherine Ross' characters *end* the movie at the back of a bus with the famous "what now?" shot, where the fate of their relationship is completely uncertain. Walter and Lila's relationship *begins* at the back of a bus, with Walter taking the seat next to Lila and Pakula letting Smith steal the scene by pulling the focus to her reactions at Walter's intrusive arrival. Walter might not mean to invade her space but from the moment he sits down and starts twisting around, trying to take off his backpack, he's a traveler's worst nightmare. Despite the close quarters and the film being about Walter up to this point, it's Smith who gets to carry the scene, her face completely unobscured while Walter keeps looking down and moving, or having his face hidden beneath his straw hat. Her discomfort is palpable (and understandable given the circumstances), yet other than reacting when Walter spills his canteen of water over her skirt, she doesn't make him feel worse by saying anything.

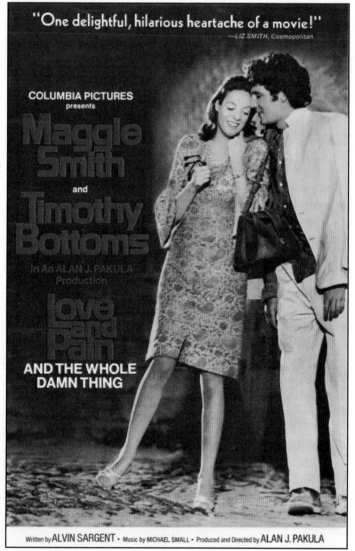

Like Walter, Lila can't catch a break. Whether it's getting her neighbors to put the right person on the phone when she calls or turning down the advances of a man obsessed with making bird calls (Emiliano Redondo), Lila makes a point of putting people down gently, and that takes effort. Lila is also on the clumsy side, which gives Smith another chance to show off her physical comedy skills, especially in the moments where Lila tries to save face. At one point she is stuck in a porta potty and tries to exit the stall with her dignity intact. Instead, she winds up tangled in the toilet paper that's stuck to her shoe, while Walter tries to help and only makes matters worse.

That Walter and Lila will become a romantic item isn't obvious, but because Smith and Bottoms never try to telegraph their romance or curb the awkwardness of their interactions, it gives the characters time to figure out who they are to each other, and for their relationship to change. As a film about misfits coming together and finding acceptance, *Love and Pain and the Whole Damn Thing* is the real deal - a genuine love story filled with sincerity and connection that couldn't be more tonally different from Smith's next film project, *Murder by Death* (1976).

Written by Neil Simon and directed by Robert Moore, *Murder by Death* is a big-cast murder mystery spoof in

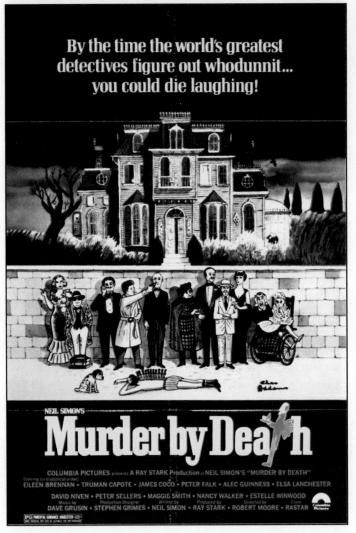

which Smith shares most of her scenes with David Niven. Lionel Twain (Truman Capote) has invited some of the most prominent detectives in the world to his home for dinner and a murder. There's Sam Diamond (Peter Falk, doing his best Humphrey Bogart as Sam Spade impression), Sidney Wang (Peter Sellers in the Charlie Chan role), Jessica Marbles (Elsa Lancaster as a Miss Marple-type) and Milo Perrier (James Coco as a Poirot stand-in). Smith and Niven are Dick and Dora Charleston, a thinly veiled send up of *The Thin Man*'s Nick and Nora Charles. They even have a dog named Myron instead of Asta.

Going by the address on Dick and Dora's invitation, the Charlestons live in New York, which is where Nick and Nora stayed in the first *Thin Man*, but it seems like an unnecessary detail to retain, especially since Smith and Niven are both British and it would've made more sense to have them be from the UK.

The same goes for Peter Sellers being cast as Charlie Chan. While Charlie Chan has often been played by white actors in yellowface, that doesn't mean the film couldn't have satirized the character and still cast an Asian actor in the role.

Being politically correct isn't really *Murder by Death*'s bag, though. While Alec Guinness is clearly channeling his Ealing comedy days, his blind butler induces some cringes. Neither Niven nor Smith are given much to do (Smith even less so as the wife of one of the detectives).

As anyone who's seen *Downton Abbey* knows, Smith is a master at delivering zingers and she gets to deliver a few good ones here (including "Why would anybody want to steal a dead, naked body?"), but since it's an ensemble cast there's not much time to explore Dick and Dora's implied marital problems. In *The Thin Man* movies, too, Nora was always the one encouraging Nick's detective work (to the point that Nick locks Nora in a closet in *After the Thin Man* to keep her from joining the investigation), so it's strange to see Dora be so apathetic here, looking for any excuse to get them out of working the case.

The two best scenes are Dick and Dora's first scene (where they're lost in the fog yet somehow have martinis on hand) and their stiff upper lip response to finding a deadly scorpion in their bed, but whether they're worth sticking the film out depends on your taste in comedy.

For a more traditional murder mystery, John Guillermin's *Death on the Nile* (1978) is based on the Agatha Christie book of the same name and follows Hercules Poirot (Peter Ustinov) as he tries to investigate a murder aboard a steamboat in Egypt. Smith plays one of the suspects, Bowers, who is aboard as a companion to Bette Davis' Miss Van Schuyler.

Mia Farrow (always in her element as a character

teetering on the brink of madness) and Angela Lansbury (as a dotty romance writer who keeps calling Poirot 'Monsieur Porridge') might have the plum parts in this star-studded cast, but Smith holds her own, especially in her scenes with Davis. It's hard to imagine an employee resenting her employer more than Bowers resents Miss Van Schuyler, and because they're able to get at each other's goats there's a prickliness to all their interactions that's delightful. It's almost easy to forget that Bowers is a nurse (until she's asked to attend to one of the other guests) because of how impatient she is with Miss Van Schuyler.

Later in the film it's revealed that Bowers wasn't always

a domestic but was born into a wealthy family. That backstory, though, can be found in how Bowers carries herself from the start of the movie. Smith is a genius at using body language to inform character, and the way she yanks and grabs at Davis, shows how little she cares about keeping her true feelings a secret. Unlike Jane Birkin, who plays Lois Chiles' servant in the film, Bowers' class status doesn't show in the clothes she wears either. During a night out she even wears a suit like Marlene Dietrich's which, combined with some comments made by Miss Van Schuyler, provides some gay subtext.

Smith's last film of the decade and second Oscar win (this time for Supporting Actress) came courtesy of Herbert Ross' *California Suite* (1978). Featuring a screenplay by Neil Simon, *California Suite* is an anthology film but one with an unusual structure. Technically it can be divided into four segments, with Smith appearing in the *Visitors from London* episode alongside Michael Caine but, initially, the film jumps around between the four. The stories never really overlap. What connects them is setting - all the characters are visitors to L.A. - but suddenly, after jumping around, the film devotes a huge chunk of time to the *Visitors from New York*, starring Jane Fonda and Alan Alda. Their segment is the wordiest, with dialogue that would be better suited for a play than a film. It's hard to

figure out where they stand with each other, the language is so thick and impenetrable.

Smith and Caine make a much better go at it in their segment, with Smith playing an actress named Diana whose been nominated for an Academy Award (unlike Smith in real life, she doesn't win). Caine is her husband, Sidney, who's come along for the ceremony. For those used to seeing stars with hair and make-up teams, there's a surprising lack of glitz to Diana's preparations. In fact,

one of the biggest takeaways from their segment is how unglamorous Diana's life is. At one point after the ceremony Diana even pinches scraps from other guests' room service trays because the kitchen is closed and can't serve an omelette.

While Smith and Caine are playing characters, there's plenty of namedropping of real movie stars (including David Niven, Smith's co-star from *Murder by Death* and *Death on the Nile*). The film opens, for example, with a scene from the film Diana has been nominated for, a lowbrow comedy where her co-star is James Coburn (playing himself) and they're on an airplane that's about to crash. Diana is watching the film as her in-flight movie and, if it wasn't clear from the clip, Diana expresses bewilderment herself at why, of all the prestigious roles she's played, this is the one she's being recognized for.

As the night goes on, it becomes apparent that Diana isn't feeling very secure about her marriage (and as she gets more drunk, she becomes more direct with her suspicions). Through all the bickering and fighting, though, Caine and Smith never lose sight of the fondness Diana and Sidney have for each other. It pervades through all their scenes together. No matter how many jokes Sidney tells at Diana's expense (and they always hit the mark with deadly accuracy), there's love there. Selling a dry sense of humor is a balancing act, and Caine is able to ensure his one-liners are cutting and brutal, not cruel, while Smith dishes back everything he serves (she even throws an apple at him in one scene). Diana may be frustrated with her husband, but she stands her ground, and eventually

Sidney gives her some straight answers. Smith's career, likewise, continues to flourish. In fact, I'd go so far as to say there's nothing the actress (now *Dame* Maggie Smith to use her proper title) can't play.

MARATHON MAN
Running from Fear

by James Cadman

Marathon Man is one of the best examples of the paranoid thriller, the genre moulded by the political and social turbulence of Vietnam and Watergate in '70s America. Others belonging to the genre include *The Parallax View* (1974), *Three Days of the Condor* (1975) and *All the President's Men* (1976). All were popular with jittery audiences who remained wary of authority, not least governmental institutions perceived to be caught up in dark conspiracies centred around a nefarious 'deep state'.

After the commercial disappointment of *The Day of the Locust*, British director John Schlesinger was looking for a hit - something that would attract the crowds who had flocked to *The Godfather*, *The Exorcist* and *Jaws*. By 1976, Schlesinger was exactly halfway into his 48-year career and *Marathon Man* marked his first foray into the thriller genre. With the financial backing of the mighty Robert Evans and the writing prowess of William Goldman, he had a guaranteed winner. It went on to gross more than $20 million in North America alone.

The story, adapted by Goldman from his 1974 novel, hinges on a cache of diamonds held in a safety deposit box in a New York City bank. As the opening titles roll, we see an elderly German man visiting the bank and, after exchanging items with a passer-by, climbing into his car to join the morning traffic. In a somewhat eccentric sequence, we then witness him becoming embroiled in a form of road rage with an angry Jewish motorist. What feels like an amusing moment soon turns dark, as both cars slam into a fuel truck, killing the two men instantly in a huge fireball. Through the flames, a crowd of onlookers surveys the carnage.

One of the onlookers is Babe Levy, the 'marathon man'

of the title, played with great energy by Dustin Hoffman. We were introduced to him moments earlier in one of his regular stints jogging around Central Park. A keen runner, Babe is something of a loner - a Columbia University student haunted by the suicide of his blacklisted father in the wake of the Red Scare of the '50s. We later see him awkwardly pursuing a romance with mysterious fellow student Elsa (Marthe Keller) who claims to be Swiss.

The action shifts to Paris and we are introduced to what appears to be an American spy by the name of Scylla (a trim and chiselled Roy Scheider). His exploits are unclear, but we see him narrowly escaping several attempts on his life as he interacts with numerous agents and assassins. Through all the apparent espionage, we learn there are two things linking Scylla to New York: one, a cache of diamonds; two, the fact that he has a brother - Babe.

Scylla and his associates know the diamonds belong to a dangerous Nazi war criminal, Dr Christian Szell (a wonderfully evil Laurence Olivier). Prompted by the death of his brother (the elderly German killed in the fiery road accident at the start of the pic), Szell comes out of hiding and travels to New York to retrieve his fortune. A former dentist in the concentration camps, Szell bought the diamonds with the gold he extracted from the mouths of his Jewish prisoners.

Back in New York, Babe and Elsa have become lovers. One night, as they stroll through Central Park, they are targeted by two unlikely, well-dressed muggers. On hearing the news, Scylla (known to his brother as Doc) arrives in Babe's apartment and, after a brief reunion, later returns covered in blood, collapsing and dying in Babe's arms. The unexpected, fatal wound was administered by

Szell and, with Doc dead and Szell fearing his plans may be thwarted, Babe soon becomes a target.

If the plot feels somewhat disjointed, the film really scores as a collection of stand-out moments. It is the impressive craftsmanship of some of the finest in the business that make these scenes so memorable. Let's explore them, one-by-one.

Doc, who turns out to be a covert diamond courier, is attacked in his Paris hotel room. In a very creepy visual, we see him standing on the balcony looking down on the street below. Behind him, a net curtain blows in the wind and is shown fluttering over the staring face of his would-be killer. As with other moments in the film, the violence is sudden and brutal, with editor Jim Clark capturing the blood spurting from Scheider's hand as he tries to stop himself being strangled with a garrote wire. After taking part in rehearsals, where the fight felt too staged and far-fetched, Scheider and actor James Wing Woo (playing the assassin) set about choreographing the moves themselves and the result is a terrific scene.

When Doc travels to New York to be with his brother, we witness a pivotal moment in the plot when he takes Babe and Elsa out for lunch in an upmarket restaurant. Goldman's superb dialogue manipulates the audience with light banter turning to suspicion and powerful emotion when Doc reveals his suspicions that Elsa is in fact German.

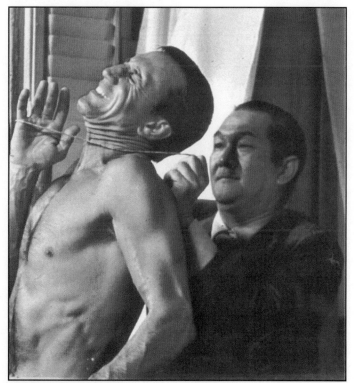

A little more 'in the know', the audience shares in Babe's confusion and desire to know the truth. This short scene is a masterclass, with Hoffman, Keller and Scheider all at the top of their game.

Perhaps most famous of all is the dental torture scene, brilliantly lit by Conrad Hall. Pinned to a chair by Szell's goons (the menacing Marc Lawrence and Richard Bright), Babe is subjected to some unwanted dental work at the hands of the sadistic Nazi. Goldman originally planned for Babe to be suffering from toothache early in the story, thinking it would make the torture even more unbearable. He asked his periodontist ("a genuinely kind and decent human being") for advice and the doctor suggested that Szell should drill into a healthy tooth, describing with disturbing relish how "the level of agony would be unsurpassable. Death would be preferable. The memory of being destroyed in the chair would never leave you." During test screenings, the scene was met with so much revulsion that Schlesinger decided to remove some of Jim Clark's grisliest footage. Olivier's decision to play the scene with real care and precision only adds to the tension. The day of the shoot, he had observed a gardener cutting roses at Evans' guest cottage. Admiring the delicacy of his craft, he decided he would emulate this style for the scene. What makes the moment so disturbing is that it's relatable. Other torture scenes can shock but often the tools or method are unfamiliar to the audience. Goldman describes the effect perfectly: "The dentist meant fear, just like in *Psycho*, in the shower scene, that meant fear. There was something unconsciously terrifying about taking a shower with a curtain drawn, and it was the same with a dentist. You never knew what might happen next." More than forty-five years on from the film's release, it still makes for unsettling viewing.

There are several shots that benefit from the use of Garrett Brown's pioneering Steadicam system. Perhaps one of the best examples is when, after being tortured, Babe evades capture and runs out onto the dark, desolate streets. Disorientated, he is seen running along half naked with the villains in hot pursuit. Shot on location in Lower Manhattan, it took nine nights to film. Amusingly, during one of the takes, one of the villains (played by William Devane) chases Babe over a pile of dirt. Reaching for Hoffman, Devane got too close and accidentally pulled down the star's pyjama bottoms, exposing his bare bottom to onlookers! The Steadicam works brilliantly as it tracks Devane's desperate attempts to catch up with Hoffman ("Get the fucking car!" he snarls to an accomplice). It is a thrilling sequence. Although *Marathon Man* was the first theatrically released film to feature the device, it had already been used on Hal Ashby's *Bound for Glory* (released two months after *Marathon Man*).

Without doubt, Michael Small's bone-chilling score only adds to the looming fear; his frantic strings and screaming synthesisers are a perfect accompaniment to the nightmarish imagery, lending a sense of existentialist horror to the film.

As a teenager, I was a huge fan of the horror genre. Among my clearest memories from the '90s was the many enthusiastic conversations with my fellow classmates about the latest slasher videos to hit the shelves. We must have seen them all. One film I remember owning on VHS was the popular 1984 documentary *Terror*

in the Aisles. Grossing $10m at box office in its own right, it called itself "A non-stop rollercoaster ride through the scariest moments of the greatest terror films of all time." Clips from *Marathon Man* were among the segments edited into the compilation. Another horror compilation was produced for the 2010 Oscars ceremony which included a clip of the famous dental torture scene. Rather than taking to social media to comment on the designer outfits gracing the red carpet, people instead questioned whether *Marathon Man* should really be considered a horror film.

What cannot be disputed is that horror is a genre that seeks to provoke fear in its audience for entertainment purposes. Thinking back to my teenage years, one of the

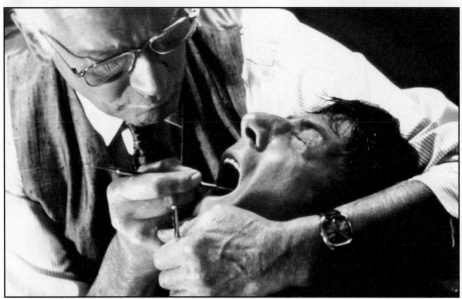

first books I remember owning on the topic was the simply titled 'Horror', a critical assessment of horror film and literature by the author and poet Leonard Wolf. In his introduction, Wolf observes that "there is an admirable thriftiness in human nature that prompts us to make even of fear a source of pleasure. Because in its grip we feel vividly alive." With *Marathon Man*, Schlesinger sought to create a film about "fear and pain... and the endurance of pain" and he certainly succeeded.

Schlesinger considered that, at 38, Hoffman was too old to play the central role of college student Babe (the character was supposed to be 24). Evans insisted on casting Hoffman who does a fine job embodying the powerlessness and vulnerability that echoed through society at the time. Years later, Hoffman's biographer, Ronald Bergan, would question how Al Pacino (three years Hoffman's junior) would have handled the role. Hoffman comes across "warm and extrovert", while Pacino typically comes across "cooler and more introverted." Since the film is overheated in its style, Bergan ponders if Pacino may have "thrown some much-needed cold water on it." Despite Schlesinger's passion for detail, we don't learn enough about Babe's character to really care (even the backstory involving his efforts to clear his father's name, preparing a thesis on the abuse of power in the history of American politics, is never fully explored and only subtly linked to present day events). Goldman felt his hero needed to be "a total innocent," and was particularly intrigued by the question: "What if someone close to you was something totally different from what you thought?" As a result, we find ourselves much more interested in the intrigue surrounding Scheider's James Bond-style exploits in Europe.

Fresh from his success in *Jaws*, Scheider gives an assured performance as the cool, confident Doc. Fans of the film have expressed their disappointment at Schlesinger's decision to remove a violent sequence which would have been our first glimpse of Scheider's character. In the scene, Doc meets a veteran agent at an airport bar. The gentleman is aging and knows he is 'on the way out.' When he goes to the toilet and fails to return, Doc goes to investigate and finds that he's been killed. He loses control and kills the two assassins. For Goldman, this was a grievous cut, as the scene would have served to establish Doc's own vulnerability, showing him as "a guy who's dead but won't lie down" and lending his scenes with Babe a stronger emotional subtext. "Without that eight-and-a-half-minute scene, you see a superstud," Goldman claimed.

Richard Widmark was originally considered for the role of Szell and even auditioned for the part in London. Goldman was especially impressed with Widmark. It appeared unlikely that Evans would achieve his goal of casting Olivier because in the months leading up to filming the great actor's health had declined considerably. He was suffering with cancer and his condition was affecting his ability to walk and even impacting his speech. With most of the filming taking place in the United States, Evans had to fight hard to be able to insure Olivier and finally succeeded in persuading Lloyd's of London to provide six weeks of insurance cover.

Much has been written about the legendary on-set banter between Hoffman and Olivier. In his 1994 biography 'The Kid Stays in the Picture', producer Robert Evans described them as a "rhapsody of opposites." Schlesinger discovered that Hoffman liked to improvise, to discover new approaches to a scene, but Olivier preferred to memorise the script as written and to remain faithful to it. Ever the unwavering method actor, Hoffman would build up a sweat by running miles between takes so he could 'become' Babe. To look 'out of it' during the notorious torture scene, he went days without sleep - so much so that when Schlesinger reviewed the rushes Hoffman's eyes appeared void of expression. Frustrated that he would have to reshoot part of the scene, Olivier famously asked: "Why doesn't he just try acting?"

Olivier's portrayal of Szell is a tour-de-force of villainy. In another nod to James Bond, he even has a retractable blade up his coat sleeve which he uses to despatch his victims with cold-blooded restraint. The Nazi war criminal was inspired by the real-life Dr. Josef Mengele who Goldman saw as "the most intellectually startling of the Nazis." Still alive when the film was made, hiding in Paraguay, Mengele

had conducted ghastly medical experiments on prisoners at Auschwitz during World War II. Interestingly, Olivier would go on to portray almost the complete opposite of Szell, a Jewish Nazi hunter on the trail of none other than Josef Mengele, in Franklin J Schaffner's *The Boys from Brazil* (1978). While not as effective as *Marathon Man*, it works well as a companion piece to Schlesinger's film, and I recommend seeking it out.

In researching this article, I was genuinely moved to see the huge respect and admiration the entire cast and crew had for Olivier. Schlesinger recalled how delighted everyone was to see his health improving with every new day. In an emotional send-off when the filming had wrapped, Hoffman called him "a great soldier... an important artist." A rhapsody of opposites, maybe, but they work superbly together in *Marathon Man* to create a splendid thriller.

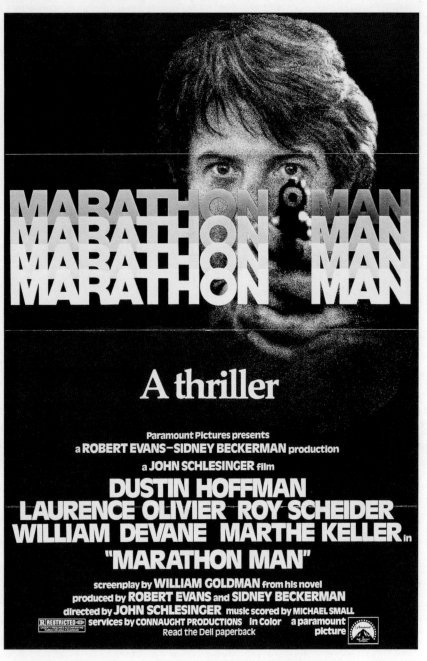

Buckling Up for a Wild Ride with

Mother, Jugs & Speed

by John Harrison

"Thanks to muggings, malnutrition, assassination and disease, we got a chance to make a buck!" - Harry 'Doughnut' Fishbine.

The '60s saw young Americans try to push their country towards a path of peace and sharing, finding meaning and richness in knowledge and helping others rather than possessions and financial status. By the mid '70s, that ethos had crumbled under the weight of instinctive human greed, and the 'Me Generation' had well and truly kicked in. Profit over people became the mantra for most businesses and services, even in the health sector (an industry once known for compassion and caring but now motivated by

dollars and cents like everything else). Set amongst the privatised world of independent ambulance services, Peter Yates' black comedy *Mother, Jugs & Speed* (1976) provides a powerfully damning yet very funny comment on the sorry state of America's health system at the time (which, many might say, has improved little since).

'Mother' Tucker (Bill Cosby) is the star driver for the Los Angeles-based F+B Ambulance Company, a small outfit locked in a fierce competition with another provider, Unity

Ambulance, to try and win a city contract. Run by the unscrupulous Harry 'Doughnut' Fishbine (Allen Garfield), the F+B crews are not above slashing the tyres on the Unity Ambulance vehicles, hiding evidence of drug use or slipping the cops a few bucks, if it means claiming a job ahead of their rivals. While excellent behind the wheel, Mother is a jaded, cynical character who drinks on the job and takes pleasure in frightening the life out of the local nuns with the ambulance siren. His riding partner is the perpetually stoned Leroy (Bruce Davison), a '60s burn-out questioning his life and where it is heading.

Also working for the F+B company are John Murdoch (Larry Hagman), a super-sleazy and oversexed driver who tries it on with just about every lady who gets wheeled into the back of his ambulance (including an unconscious overdose case) and Jennifer (Raquel Welch), the switchboard operator whom her male co-workers have charmingly nicknamed 'Jugs', for reasons that should be obvious to anyone familiar with Welch's physical attributes. Coming into this band of misfits and miscreants is a new driver, Tony Malatesta (Harvey Keitel), a sheriff's detective and Vietnam War ambulance driver whom Mother nicknames 'Speed' after hearing he had been suspended by the sheriff's office following allegations that he sold cocaine to young teenagers. When Jennifer reveals that she has secretly been studying for her own ambulance license and EMT (Emergency Medical Technician) certificate and wants to progress away from the switchboard, Tony is the only one who takes her seriously and the pair become intimate, much to the jealousy of Murdoch and some of the other drivers. While 'Mother' tries to gleefully throw Jennifer into the deep end, making her deal with an overweight patient who has gotten himself caught in his zipper, she proves herself more than capable at her job, though she begins to have doubts when a pregnant mother in her care bleeds to death in the back of the ambulance.

When the city ends up awarding the contract to a third independent ambulance provider, Unity's owner suggests they merge with F+B, a suggestion which Fishbine initially rejects. The discussions at City Hall are broken up by news that an intoxicated and armed Murdoch has gone berserk and taken Mrs. Fishbine (Valerie Curtin) hostage back at the garage. After the ambulance drivers race back to try and diffuse the scene, 'Speed' is shot in the shoulder and Murdoch is shot and killed by a police officer when he takes aim at 'Mother' (though it's revealed his gun was empty). In the aftermath of the shooting, Fishbine agrees to merge F+B with Unity, and 'Speed', now cleared of his drug charges, is allowed to return to the police force, though he and Jennifer remain involved. Having proven her worth in the field, 'Mother' insists that Jennifer be his new partner, and the pair set off in their ambulance to terrorize some nuns.

The idea for *Mother, Jugs & Speed* began in the mind of Joseph Barbera, one half of the legendary cartoon-creating duo of Hanna-Barbera, who thought a film about ambulance drivers could make for an interesting story. He pitched his concept to 20th Century Fox, who went for the idea and hired Tom Mankiewicz to develop a screenplay. Mankiewicz had hit something of a career purple patch, having written (or co-written) the three most recent Bond films, *Diamonds Are Forever* (1971), *Live and Let Die* (1973) and *The Man with the Golden Gun* (1974). Mankiewicz made the screenplay to *Mother, Jugs & Speed* pretty much his own, filling it with his identifiable brand of characters, dialogue and humour, though Barbera remained on-board as an executive producer.

With Mankiewicz's screenplay veering between comedy, social satire and bleak drama, *Mother, Jugs & Speed* is brought to life by the actors chosen to play their respective characters. Gene Hackman was initially approached to play the role of 'Mother' Tucker, which certainly would've been an interesting choice and would have changed the tone of the film drastically. Hackman was exhausted, having just come off Stanley Donen's *Lucky Lady* (1975), so he passed on the project but suggested Bill Cosby as an alternative. Cosby and Mankiewicz clearly played around with the screenplay and character to suit the comedian's style and humour. Cosby at the time was still riding a wave of popularity, particularly amongst children, thanks to his participation in the animated series *Fat Albert and the Cosby Kids* (which Cosby created and appeared in via live-action wraparound segments) and *The Electric Company* (a spin-off of *Sesame Street* aimed at slightly older kids). The part of Jennifer was first offered to Valerie Perrine, but she declined as she would not accept the deferred payment the producers were offering to help offset the film's low budget (deferred payment is, of course, an agreement to pay at a later date, usually once the film is out and generating revenue). Perrine was an actress on the rise at the time, coming off her performance in *Lenny* (1974), but Raquel Welch was a bona fide superstar in 1976, and probably at the height of her physical beauty.* As breathtaking as Welch looks in *Mother, Jugs & Speed* (her character is dressed in attire which firmly emphasizes the reason why she has been given the nickname 'Jugs'), her performance goes beyond the superficial and she imbues Jennifer with some genuine emotion. You can feel and believe the harassment and condescending attitude she receives (mostly from men, of course), yet Welch doesn't play the role for sympathy. There is a strength to her which offsets her vulnerability, making her character a very interesting one to watch develop. As 'Speed', it's interesting to see a young Keitel breaking out from his work with Martin Scorsese.

While all three leads deliver excellent performances, it's Larry Hagman who creates the biggest impression, and seems to have the best handle on his character and material. Hagman was in between his two iconic television roles, Major Anthony Nelson on the fantasy sitcom *I Dream of Jeannie* (1965-1970) and ruthless oil tycoon J. R. Ewing in the prime-time soap drama *Dallas* (1978-1991). No doubt keen to break free of the nervy and perplexed Major Nelson, Hagman kept himself fairly busy during the first half of the '70s showing up on *Rod Serling's Night Gallery* (1970) and in TV movies like the atmospheric genre piece *A Howling in the Woods* (1971), where he re-united

*Two years after *Mother, Jugs & Speed*, both Hackman and Perrine would find themselves working together on *Superman: The Movie* (1978) and its sequel *Superman II* (1980), demonstrating a clear onscreen chemistry with each other.

with his *Jeannie* co-star Barbara Eden. Hagman's strangest credit during this period was as the director of low-budget horror comedy sequel *Beware! The Blob* (1972, aka *Son of Blob*).** He really is very funny in *Mother, Jugs & Speed*, not to mention genuinely creepy in the way he sleazes onto women while performing his duty. He also brings an underlying complexity to his personality, which comes to the fore when he suffers his mental breakdown during the climax.

Featured amongst the intriguing support cast is Toni Basil, who makes a brief but very memorable appearance as an unnamed junkie who, in the grip of a terrible withdrawal and in desperate need of a fix, calls 'Mother' and Leroy out to her house by a dock with the intention of robbing them at gunpoint of any drugs they may have in their ambulance. It all goes horribly, very violently wrong, resulting in one of *Mother, Jugs & Speed*'s most jarring and shocking moments. Looking pale and sweaty, dark rings circling her wide eyes, Basil brings her character to life with a potent combination of on-edge desperation and vulnerability. Basil's unique career began as a choreographer and dancer in Elvis, beach party and teen movies in the '60s, before appearing in the counterculture classics *Head* (1967) and *Easy Rider* (1969), as well as Bob Rafelson's devastating American drama *Five Easy Pieces* (1970). A few years after *Mother, Jugs & Speed*, Basil began to focus more on her career as a recording artist and live performer, which culminated in her 1981 album *Word of Mouth*, a true new

wave/pop gem that spawned the infectious, worldwide hit single *Mickey*. As the '80s progressed, Basil would return to film, starring in two horror films which played somewhat on her musical personality, *Slaughterhouse Rock* (1988) and *Rockula* (1990), and playing a flamboyant art gallery owner in the exploitation film *Angel III: The Final Chapter* (1988), the third entry in the popular series about the "High school honour student by day, Hollywood hooker by night". (You can read more about her career in the interview I conducted with her in 'Shock Cinema' #60 or via her authorised website www.tonibasil.net).

Another familiar face who shows up in *Mother, Jugs & Speed* is the great actor/director L. Q. Jones, a favourite of Sam Peckinpah, who plays Sheriff Davey, always happy to give 'Mother' a tip on a fresh body in return for a fin (or fiver) in his hand. And Bruce Davison provides another very solid performance as the doomed Leroy. What a terrific and varied film career Davison has enjoyed over the decades. Real-life wrestler Barbie Dahl plays the blonde wrestler who Murdoch tries to sleaze on after she is thrown by her opponent out of the ring and onto a row of chairs. Initially the legendary Fabulous Moolah was scheduled to play the part, but she was forced to pull out due to a gallbladder infection. Another real-life sportsperson, American NFL player Dick Butkus, who was a linebacker for the Chicago Bears between 1965-1973, plays brash Texan ambulance driver 'Rodeo' Moxey.

Eschewing a traditional soundtrack score, *Mother, Jugs*

**After Hagman found superstardom as J. R. Ewing, and *Dallas* had its infamous "Who shot J.R.?" plotline from 1980, *Beware! The Blob* was re-issued in America with the creative tagline of "The movie J.R. shot!"

Speed instead fills its aural spaces with a superb selection of pop, soul-funk and rock tracks. From the bumping disco-fied funk of Paul Jabara's *Dance*, which busts out during the film's opening credits, to Peter Frampton's *Show Me the Way*, playing on a stereo in the background while 'Mother' and Leroy talk to a smacked-out junkie about the boy lying dead of an overdose in her bed, the soundtrack to *Mother, Jugs & Speed* forms an integral part of the film's tone and appeal. Also featuring tracks by Steve Marriott, Billy Preston and Michelle Phillips, the soundtrack was issued at the time on the A&M Records label.

Mother, Jugs & Speed was a mid-career film from English director Peter Yates, who had cut his teeth in the '60s on episodes of the action/spy shows *The Saint* and *Danger Man*, not to mention the classic pop musical *Summer Holiday* (1963) starring Cliff Richard, and the crime thriller *Robbery* (1967) with Stanley Baker. The latter, a fictionalised account of the infamous Great Train Robbery of 1963, no doubt helped Yates to land the job directing Steve McQueen in the ground-breaking American action thriller *Bullitt* (1968), a film which really helped modernise that genre, and created a template that is still being used today. Yates followed up *Mother, Jugs & Speed* with the underwater thriller *The Deep* (1978), before moving on to the excellent coming-of-age comedy drama *Breaking Away* (1979), for which he received an Oscar nomination. His eclectic career continued in the '80s with *Eyewitness* (1981), *Krull* (1983), *The Dresser* (1983) (which garnered him a second Oscar nod), *Suspect* (1987) and *An Innocent Man* (1989). A solid journeyman director who often went where the work was, Yates' career finished with a run of comedy dramas and Hallmark TV movies in the '90s and early 2000s, before he passed away in 2011 at the age of 81.

Very much a film of its time, particularly in its sexual attitudes and mores, newer viewers hoping to appreciate *Mother, Jugs & Speed* will likely need to separate the art from the artist, given what we now know about Bill Cosby and his horrific predatory behaviour over the decades. The Cosby factor and how to deal with it is likely one of the main reasons why there has not been any kind of decent home video release of the film (another issue could be music clearance rights for the soundtrack). There have been VHS releases in the '80s, of course, and a DVD issued by 20th Century Fox in 2004, before Cosby's acts were publicly exposed. The DVD release does contain a few trailers and TV spots for the film, as well as a selection of Raquel Welch trailers, but it's a film that could well use a digital upgrade and some

Alan J. Pakula
Forgotten Master Filmmaker of the '70s

by John H. Foote

"He had an affinity with women," said Jane Fonda, speaking of the writer-producer-director Alan J. Pakula. "He understood us, and appreciated us, and I loved the way he made us part of the collaboration. He was a special man."

Meryl Streep said: "Alan was remarkable, just a remarkable man. So gentle and loving in his guiding the actors, with such a clear vision. I adored him."

Both actresses, legends, won Academy Awards under the direction Pakula. Fonda's was for her role as a tough but vulnerable hooker in *Klute* (1971), a ground-breaking performance that opened the door for women to be realistic in the '70s. Eleven years later, Streep won her first Best Actress Oscar for her astonishing performance in Pakula's *Sophie's Choice* (1982), in which she portrayed a Holocaust survivor who prevailed by making a dreadful choice which still haunts her years after the war. It might be the greatest screen performance ever given by an actress. Streep is miraculous in the role.

Alan J. Pakula. How is it the director of such '70s and '80s masterpieces as *Klute* (1971), *All the President's Men* (1976) and *Sophie's Choice* (1982) is not more greatly appreciated or respected as a filmmaker today?

When I interviewed actor-director George Clooney at the Toronto International Film Festival a few years ago, I asked him directly which directors have had the greatest influence on him as a director. Without hesitation he answered: "Pakula! Alan Pakula." Clooney cited Hal Ashby and Sidney Lumet too, but Pakula's name came out of his mouth first, without hesitation. He is not alone - many

of the top directors working today have mentioned being influenced by the director, including David Fincher whose film *Zodiac* (2007) felt for all the world like *All the President's Man*, one of the finest films of the '70s and, indeed, a contender for the very best movie about journalism from any decade.

Despite his gifts as a filmmaker, Pakula did not begin his career in the director's chair. Instead, he started out behind the scenes, producing films for his friend Robert Mulligan. In 1962 they gave us the instant classic *To Kill a Mockingbird*, a superb adaptation of the great Harper Lee book. Gregory Peck was never better than here as the decent, kind Atticus Finch, winning a Best Actor Oscar for his masterly portrayal. It would be another seven years before Pakula decided to direct a film himself and when he did, he displayed great talent and a natural way with actors.

His *The Sterile Cuckoo* (1969) depicts a quirky romance between two outsiders trying to fit in as they move into college. Pookie (Liza Minnelli) proves to have intense emotional troubles which manifest themselves as the couple become ever closer after intimacy. In her first major role, Minnelli proves herself, like her mother, a gifted and natural actress. The credit for that must go to Pakula for drawing such a fine performance out of her. For the film, Minnelli was awarded an Academy Award nomination and Pakula received excellent reviews, in particular for his expert guidance of the young actors.

His second film is a masterpiece of noir and paranoia. Jane Fonda's Bree Daniels is a sometimes-actress, most-times hooker who is being stalked by a predator who means her harm. John Klute is the name of the cop who comes to her aid. His surname is also the name of the film. Played by Donald Sutherland, he is the towering man Bree clings to for protection, gradually falling in love with him. Both actors are superb, and there is an exciting, dangerous performance from Roy Scheider as Bree's pimp, though Fonda received the lion's share of great reviews. And why not? Her performance is electrifying, her confidence onscreen shocking, her vulnerability heartbreaking. We come to see Bree as one tough lady, but that doesn't stop her becoming as terrified as a little girl looking for monsters under her bed when this man, this stalker, begins to threaten her safety.

Fonda won an Academy Award for Best Actress at a time when her politics did not endear her to the American people or the fickle Academy. After sweeping the major film awards, there was no way the Academy could deny her. Previous to the Oscar, she had won the Golden Globe, the New York Film Critics award, and the National Society of Film Critics award. In each acceptance speech, she thanked Pakula for his artistry. But upon winning the Oscar, she was brief, stating simply: "There is a lot to say,

but tonight is not the time to say it. Thank you." It was perfect and Pakula understood completely the intense pressure the actress was under.

Klute is notable for the manner in which the director allows the actress to take center stage and hold the film together with her superb performance. The camera often lingers on Fonda's face as we watch her move through a plethora of emotions, the actress always serving the story. She fearlessly makes her sex scenes near comic, looking at her watch while making love to a client, obviously feeling nothing, more concerned about checking the time and getting the hell out of there. There is, however, nothing false about her relationship with Klute, beautifully portrayed by Sutherland (her real-life lover for a time). Fonda gives an extraordinary performance, among the finest ever captured on film.

Soon after, Pakula helmed the political thriller *The Parallax View* (1974) which deals openly and powerfully with assassinations influenced by the findings of the controversial Warren Report and the recent paranoia in Washington over Watergate. Warren Beatty gives one of his best performances in the film, which proved a solid success with audiences and critics.

His next film, though, would be his masterpiece. It is among the greatest of the decade.

All the President's Men is astonishing, brilliantly exploring the story of the reporting that would bring down President Richard Nixon, elected two years previously in the greatest landslide in American history. Working from a superb screenplay by William Goldman, who stunningly pieced together the Watergate story in chronological order, we watch transfixed as the two Washington Post reporters, Bob Woodward and Carl Bernstein - thrown together despite conflicting styles - slowly and methodically investigate, research, interview and cold call,

exploring every avenue of enquiry available to them, to track down the root of Watergate and where it came from. Remember, this was in the '70s - long before the Internet, years before the availability of instant information. The two reporters had to forge their way through false leads and tons of information to get to the heart of the story. They had an 'in' - a man known to them only as Deep Throat, a White House insider feeding them just enough information to keep them on track. Years later, Mark Felt (associate director of the FBI when the events were taking place) revealed that he was indeed Deep Throat. He is portrayed in the film by Hal Holbrook.

Pakula creates the perfect tone, delivering a first-rate thriller which grows in scale as the reporters come to realize that whatever they're researching could well bring down the presidency. Their lives are in danger; they are continually watched; their phone lines are likely tapped, and they are constantly followed. People they need to speak to have been "gotten to" before the reporters can get to them. Something so much bigger than Woodward and Bernstein is sabotaging their work.

With an editor, Ben Bradlee (Jason Robards), who believes in them, the intrepid journalists forge on, and history tells us they were right to do so. As they type up the story that will break Watergate wide open, connecting the dots to President Richard Nixon, we see election night playing on TV. Nixon has just been re-elected. The clock is ticking on him, and he knows it.

Pakula gives the film an urgency that is perfect and his casting is spot-on. Robert Redford was already a producer when Pakula was hired, and he was cast as Bob Woodward, with Dustin Hoffman coming aboard as Carl Bernstein. Much was made at the time of Hoffman's remarkable resemblance to Bernstein, though Woodward was not

blessed with Redford's good looks. Not that looks matter in this film - it's a snapshot of history, recent history at that, and Pakula shows a great sense of responsibility about getting the factual details just right.

Released in the spring, the dog days of movie releases, it was an immediate sensation, an instant hit with audiences and especially critics.

At year's end, Pakula won the New York Film Critics Award for Best Director, was a Director's Guild of America nominee, and his film was nominated for eight Academy Awards. In a year that saw an extraordinary Best Picture list, including *All the President's Men*, *Bound for Glory*, *Network*, *Rocky* and *Taxi Driver*, the least of them won Best Picture, *Rocky*. It remains a blight on the Academy that Pakula lost and that his film was not named the year's best picture. It remains the finest film ever made about reporting. Indeed, it might just be that rarest of things: a perfect film.

Pakula next directed a western, a modern one, with Jane Fonda and James Caan - *Comes a Horseman* (1978). While Fonda and Caan acquit themselves very well indeed, the best performance comes from former stuntman Richard Farnsworth, who launched his acting career with an unforgettable turn which earned him an Oscar nomination in the Best Supporting Actor category. Pakula captures the vastness of the American west, but the film moves rather slowly (which critics complained somewhat loudly about) and it never caught on with audiences despite the presence of the popular stars.

Pakula's final film of the '70s was *Starting Over* (1979), an enjoyable comedy-romance with three excellent central performances. It was widely believed that Burt Reynolds might get an Oscar nomination for his work, but alas, the nominations went instead to Jill Clayburgh (Best Actress) and Candice Bergen (Best Supporting Actress). A popular film, it won over audiences and many critics... but not all.

In the years to come, Pakula directed the flop *Roll Over* (1981) with Jane Fonda and Kris Kristofferson, about high

She was as strong as the land for which she fought.
And as vulnerable.

"Comes a Horseman"
A story of love and freedom.

A ROBERT CHARTOFF-IRWIN WINKLER Production
An ALAN J. PAKULA Film

JAMES CAAN   JANE FONDA   JASON ROBARDS
"COMES A HORSEMAN"

Music by MICHAEL SMALL   Director of Photography GORDON C. WILLIS, A.S.C.
Written by DENNIS LYNTON CLARK   Produced by GENE KIRKWOOD and DAN PAULSON
Executive Producers IRWIN WINKLER and ROBERT CHARTOFF   Directed by ALAN J. PAKULA

United Artists

For the rest of the '80s, none of his films were memorable. But he returned in 1990 with the superb legal thriller *Presumed Innocent*, drawing outstanding performances from Harrison Ford, Raul Julia and a convincingly frightened Bonnie Bedelia. *Consenting Adults* (1992) was a travesty, but he returned strongly with two box office hits - *The Pelican Brief* (1993), a star vehicle for Julia Roberts and Denzel Washington, and *The Devil's Own* (1997), a Brad Pitt and Harrison Ford starrer without the director's usual style.

While working on a film about Eleanor Roosevelt, Pakula was doing odd jobs around his home and decided to go into New York to pick up some things. Driving along the Long Island Expressway on November 19th, 1998, a piece of pipe thrown up by another vehicle came through the windshield and struck Pakula in the head. An ambulance rushed him to hospital, but he was pronounced dead.

One of cinema's finest filmmakers was gone, "removed from the world" as Meryl Streep said sadly.

Like Hal Ashby, Alan J. Pakula is often one of the tragically forgotten master filmmakers of his time. However, his work is immortal. And as long as we have film buffs and lovers of cinema and filmmakers like George Clooney revering Pakula, he too will remain forever immortal.

finance and romance, but it never took off. His next film was a work of art, *Sophie's Choice* (1982), containing my pick for the single greatest performance ever given by an actress (Meryl Streep). As he did in Klute, Pakula allowed his actress to shine as a Polish-Catholic immigrant living in Brooklyn in the immediate years after the Second World War. We learn gradually that she survived Auschwitz though she lost her entire family, including her children. The choice that haunts her, and which we see in flashback, is that she was given the choice of which child would survive, her son or her toddler daughter. See the film, I will not reveal.

Streep, like Fonda, won every Best Actress award available to her that year and, though she has enjoyed a magnificent career, I don't believe she has ever surpassed her work in the film.

Pakula was ignored for his work as a director by the Academy, a shameful move, though he was nominated for writing the Adapted Screenplay of this superb film which richly deserved to be nominated for Best Picture and Best Director. In all, *Sophie's Choice* received only five nominations when, in fact, it easily deserved ten or more. *Klute*, *Starting Over* and *Sophie's Choice* saw Pakula being stamped as a particularly fine director of women.

BURT REYNOLDS
JILL CLAYBURGH   CANDICE BERGEN

Phil Potter would like to straighten out his life... One way, or the other.

Starting Over

Four of the Apocalypse
by David Flack

Whenever the Italian director Lucio Fulci is mentioned, people automatically think of his horror films and giallos from the '70s and '80s. However, these were made relatively late in his career. A closer look at his filmography reveals he made all sorts of films in all sorts of genres earlier on. For example, he tried his hand at directing westerns - three, in fact - and I'd say all three are pretty solid. I should point out here that I'm not a big fan of Fulci's horror films. I know he has a big cult following but, for me, his horror movies aren't particularly well-written and often appear sleazy, sadistic and gory. However, he certainly had some talent and, despite what I've just said, one horror film of his that I do enjoy is *Zombie Flesh Eaters* aka *Zombi* (1979). Go figure! I also like many of his crime films, and I'm generally favourable towards his three spaghetti westerns which, while not among the very best in the genre, are perfectly decent. Fulci was more adept at making westerns than my favourite Italian director Mario Bava (whose occasional forays into the western genre left much to be desired).

The three spaghetti westerns Fulci directed were *Massacre Time* (1966), *Four of the Apocalypse* (1975) and *Silver Saddle* (1978). Interestingly, the first of these was probably the first really violent effort he ever made (though he would become synonymous with violent cinema thanks to his later gore films). The third was one of the last of the spaghetti westerns to emerge in the '60s-'70s golden era. One might argue that two other films he made - *White Fang* (1973) and *Challenge to White Fang* (1974) - also belong in the western bracket, but I

think categorising them as such isn't strictly accurate. It is the middle of his three spaghetti westerns, *Four of the Apocalypse*, that I will be discussing here.

The plot follows a gambler, a pregnant prostitute, an alcoholic and a man who claims to see the dead who become unlikely travelling companions after fleeing from prison. They set out to start a new life at the gambler's suggestion at a thriving town 200 miles away. However, they attract the attention of a ruthless and sadistic bandit leader during the course of their journey.

This is basically a western road movie which throws in violence and warmth along the way. The international cast consists of an Italian (Fabio Testi) as Stubby the gambler; two British (Lynne Frederick and Harry Baird) as Bunny the prostitute and Buck the strange, possibly insane man respectively; an American (Michael J. Pollard) as Clem, the alcoholic; and a Cuban (Tomas Milian) as Chaco, the bandit leader.

The four are thrown together in the same cell after the gambler arrives in town and is immediately locked up by a dishonest sheriff who is aware of his reputation as a cardsharp. The sheriff is also aware that a vigilante group is planning to attack his jail. We're only seven minutes into the film when Fulci gives us the attack scene, replete with bloody, gory action and plenty of gaping bullet holes in victims' bodies. The attack decimates the sheriff's men, the vigilantes and most of the prisoners. However, our four protagonists survive... as does the sheriff. Accepting a fee from Stubby, the sheriff agrees to let him go as long as he takes his three cellmates with him. The sheriff even

provides a wagon and horses for them.

The four are at first uneasy companions. It starts badly when Clem, the alcoholic, drinks the gambler's toilet water which earns him a slapping, but gradually they form a bond. Along the way, they come across a small Quaker group who offer them food and drink and to stay awhile. The Quaker leader assumes Stubby and Bunny are married and, perhaps tellingly, neither of them correct him. All four decide to move on, though Clem seems a little reluctant.

The next day, the four are shot at while celebrating Bunny's birthday by a man who introduces himself as Chaco. He wishes to join them and tries to make friends, saying he will be invaluable to them. Stubby is immediately wary but the stranger accompanies them and amuses himself by blatantly shooting birds and other wildlife along the way (these scenes look worryingly real). He seems to take a lot of pleasure from this. Things become even more violent when they are attacked by three men who, we learn, are after Chaco. He makes short work of the men, killing two and wounding the third, a sheriff. Chaco really reveals his sadistic side when he digs out the bullet from the wounded man's stomach and pins his star to the man's naked breast. Then, when he tires of this, he callously shoots the man in the head. Clearly on a high thanks to all this sadism, Chaco turns his attention to his travelling companions. He torments and ridicules them, especially Clem. He makes them partake in a drug Peyote but Stubby spits his out and so isn't really affected like the others. Stubby makes a move on Chaco but is knocked unconscious, and when he comes around he finds himself, Bunny and Buck tied up. Clem is free but is drugged and drunk. Chaco turns his attention to Bunny, raping her in an uneasy scene (especially since she is already pregnant) and this infuriates Stubby who raises his objections. Chaco answers them by deliberately standing on Stubby's testicles - ouch! Chaco then threatens to leave all three to die in the desert heat but offers Clem the chance to go with him. Clem, disgusted by the rape and roused from his drunken stupor, attempts to attack Chaco with a rock but is shot in the leg for his trouble. The ruthless bandit goes off, leaving all four to their fate.

Clem manages to free Stubby, who carries out an emergency operation to remove the bullet from his leg with the help of Buck. They then make a makeshift stretcher out of some of the wagon and trek on. It only takes a while for them to come across Chaco and his gang massacring a part of unlucky travellers. They manage to stay hidden, but Chaco becomes aware someone is there. He is distracted when one of his gang says there is a Quaker group further down the trail ready for the taking. The four arrive in time to see the Quakers who helped them earlier slaughtered - every man, woman and child. This naturally upsets them all, and Stubby vows to kill Chaco.

VERDAMMT
ZU LEBEN -
VERDAMMT
ZU STERBEN
IM ADRIA-FILMVERLEIH

showdown between Stubby and Chaco which is done quickly and violently.

All in all, this is an uneven but very watchable film with some surprising moments dotted about. The English-language version is, of course, dubbed… but despite this, the performances are effective. Fabio Testi gives the best performance, going from a carefree, slightly devious cardsharp to a heroic figure who cares about his adopted family and is totally invested in what happens to them. Lynne Frederick is also good as the hapless Bunny, basically a good person thrown a bad roll of the dice of fate. The real surprise is Michael J. Pollard as Clem. Now, as a certain esteemed co-editor of this magazine will testify (Jonathon Dabell, I'm looking at you), I'm not the biggest fan of Mr. Pollard. In fact, mostly I despise him. I find him incredibly one-note, sticking with the same old schtick since making his name in *Bonnie and Clyde* (1967). He seemed to repeat and exaggerate the approach he used there, *ad nauseam*, in every role thereafter. He was acceptable in *Bonnie and Clyde* and gave a good leading performance in *Dirty Little Billy* (1972), but in everything else he pretty much irritates the hell out of me. Thankfully, he shows unexpected acting range here in *Four of the Apocalypse* and is unexpectedly sympathetic, giving possibly his best ever performance.

Tomas Milian was a veteran star of many spaghetti westerns, Eurocrime offerings, giallos and various other films. A maverick, often volatile actor, his appearance

From here, Fulci slows down the pace. The four's encounters from here onwards alternate between moments of good fortune and moments of tragedy. The director throws in some unexpectedly warm moments, like when they end up at a virtual ghost town inhabited by a gang of drunks and outlaws. Bunny goes into labour and the outlaws show their human side, finding themselves caring and becoming involved, even running bets on whether it will be a boy or girl. There is genuine warmth in these scenes, something you don't really expect in a Fulci film. As mentioned, there is tragedy too, and Fulci manages to bring emotion to the story, getting you to genuinely care about this disparate group. There is a small scene which anticipates the kind of direction Fulci's career would follow a few years later (a scene reminiscent of something from *Zombie Flesh Eaters*), but if you haven't seen either film, I won't spoil it for you.

Four of the Apocalypse climaxes with the inevitable

UNIVERSEL EXPORT PRESENTE
DANS UN FILM DE LUCIO FULCI
FABIO TESTI TOMAS MILIAN DANS
IL ETAIT UNE FOIS…
4 DE L'apocalypse
AVEC LYNNE FREDERICK, MICHAEL J. POLLARD   eastmancolor

in this twilight year's spaghetti western gives it an extra something, though in truth he is underused and only appears in three or four scenes. The first of his scenes is the best, giving him the chance to show his cunning, arrogance and sadistic cruelty. Milian based his approach to the character on Charles Manson, and in those early scenes it really shows. Good as he is, I feel he has done better, and for all his shocking, sadistic deeds, I find that in the climatic showdown he is outwitted and dispatched a little too easily. Apart from one "How do you like it?" nasty scene, his comeuppance is too quick and comparatively tame in light of what other characters have suffered at his hands. A character like this deserves a horrible demise, but he gets off rather too lightly.

I mentioned earlier that the film has its fair share of tragedy, and this was the case in real life for two members of the cast. Harry Baird is underused as Buck, the possibly insane member of the foursome. After a particular incident, his character just disappears from the film. Now, this may have been out of necessity as this proved to be

his last film. He had been diagnosed with glaucoma which got progressively worse and he was forced to retire. He eventually went blind and died of cancer aged 73 in 2005. He appeared in numerous films from 1955. This, his final film, was his third spaghetti western. As for Lynne Frederick, hers was a tragic and short life. She was famous for being Peter Sellers' fourth wife, and when she became his widow, she inherited his fortune and shunned the rest of his family. This made her (rightly or wrongly) a very unpopular figure within the film community as well as with the press and the public. She later married (and had a very rocky relationship with) TV personality David Frost. She died in 1994, aged just 39. The cause of death was undisclosed.

All in all, *Four of the Apocalypse* is not among the very top echelons of the spaghetti western genre, but it's far from the worst. It's intriguing and effective, and I'd place it amongst the best films from Lucio Fulci's colourful directorial career.

METEOR

Sean Connery is Dr. Paul Bradley

by Bryan C. Kuriawa

During the 1970s, movies were being made against a real-world landscape ripe with endless disaster. The oil crisis, global terrorism, economic stagnation, political instability and environmental worries - it was truly the best (or worst) of all worlds.

Universal's *Airport* (1970) marked the start of the decade's cinematic disaster cycle, but it took the success of *The Poseidon Adventure* (1972) to kick everything into high gear. Everything from *The Towering Inferno* (1974) to *The Cassandra Crossing* (1976) to the various *Airport* sequels sought to cash in on the trend.

The influence was felt as far away as Japan, where studios invested in their own disaster products ('Panic films' as they were known) like *Submersion of Japan* (1973) and *Bullet Train* (1975). *Submersion* was imported to the US, where new footage featuring Lorne Greene was edited in

and it was retitled *Tidal Wave* (1975).

However, by 1979 the disaster boom had exhausted itself with audiences. Newer releases like *The Swarm*, *Beyond the Poseidon Adventure* and *City on Fire* failed commercially and received a critical panning. Younger theatergoers - infused with the thrills of *Close Encounters of the Third Kind* and *Star Wars* - weren't interested any more.

Before the genre burned out, the unlikeliest of production companies - American International Pictures (AIP) - took a chance on an apocalypse picture of its own.

"That meteor is five miles wide and it's definitely going to hit us!"

While in a sailboat race in the Gulf of Mexico, Dr. Paul Bradley (Sean Connery) is whisked away by the US coastguard. He is flown to NASA's Houston headquarters for a reunion with his former colleague, Dr. Sherwood (Karl Malden). They are taken to General Easton (Joseph Campanella), who informs them about the fate of a recent spaceflight and a grave threat now endangering the world.

During a manned expedition to Mars, *Challenger II* was re-routed to the asteroid belt to oversee a comet passing through. Unfortunately, the comet struck a larger asteroid called Orpheus. The resulting explosion destroyed *Challenger* and sent a five-mile chunk of rock, along with other pieces, speeding towards Earth.

Arriving in Washington D.C., Bradley and Sherwood attempt to convince officials that the weapons satellite *Hercules* - which carries numerous nuclear warheads in orbit around Earth - provides the best chance of stopping the meteor. However, the Americans realize their missiles alone won't be enough, so they must convince the Russian government to use their own weapons platform, *Peter the Great*, in conjunction with *Hercules*.

After the American President (Henry Fonda) acknowledges the existence of *Hercules* on TV, Russia sends Dr. Dubov (Brian Keith) and his assistant Tatiana (Natalie Wood) to the US. With less than a week remaining before the main meteor strikes, détente is needed to avert the world's end.

A big-budget production from one of Hollywood's biggest B studios, *Meteor* occupies an unusual place. With its A-list cast, Cold War peace message and a blustery Connery, it's a fascinating if run-of-the-mill disaster film.

The Arkoff formula in space.

In the '50s, AIP was one of the kings of the B-movie market. Drive-ins and theaters nationwide featured posters for *The Phantom from 10,000 Leagues* (1956), *I Was a Teenage Werewolf* (1957) or *Earth vs. the Spider* (1958). With their low budgets and cheap scares, AIP movies were the backdrop to many a teenager's date night. During the early '60s, they branched out with their Edgar Allan Poe cycle and the popular *Beach Party* series. They also made a splash with Japanese and European science fiction, importing numerous titles for theatrical and television release.

By the mid '70s - under the leadership of one of its founding members, Samuel Arkoff - AIP was still going strong. They'd made Pam Grier a household name in blaxploitation films and were graduating into A-list productions like 1977's *The Island of Dr. Moreau*. Meanwhile, films like *Frogs* (1972), *Squirm* (1976) and *Empire of the Ants* (1977) kept up the B-movie feeling of decades past.

When producer Theodore R. Parvin read a 1975 article by author Isaac Asimov about a meteor striking a major city, he became interested in developing a potential movie on the theme. He teamed up with producer Arnold Orgolini and screenwriter Edmund H. North to seek investment to get the project off the ground. After

presenting the concept to numerous studios, the group got funding from Sir Run Run Shaw of Shaw Brothers, Japan's Nippon Herald Films and AIP. Arkoff also acquired distribution rights for the film in the US.

Competing directly against the majors seemed a sure possibility. Acquiring financing was one thing but getting the production underway was to prove another.

"*If you ever reach a decision, I'll be in the bar across the street.*"

Helmed by *Poseidon Adventure*'s Ronald Neame, *Meteor* features an A-list cast who were at various junctures in their respective careers.

Connery as Bradley often seems one step away from slamming the door in someone's face and yelling: "Eat wood!" In his opening scene, he threatens the coastguard team and even risks losing his sailboat. Later, he criticizes his former boss to his face and tells Washington bigwigs to get their heads "out of shit."

Once Tatiana arrives, Bradley lightens up and becomes more stoic, trying to lower the Iron Curtain between them. Nonetheless, he still finds time to call Martin Landau's General Adlon an "asshole" when the latter doubts the existence of the meteor.

Perhaps Connery's frustrations can be traced to his particular reality at that moment. Despite critical successes in *The Man Who Would be King* (1975) and *Robin and Marian* (1976), he was no longer a major box-office draw. Many of his late '70s films had underperformed with critics and been box offices disappointments. At one point, Connery looked set to work with producer Kevin McClory on a proposed *Thunderball* remake called *Warhead* (McClory had recently won his rights battle over that 007 story), but *Warhead* would be delayed by legal snafus and wouldn't see light of day until 1983 as *Never Say Never Again*. The chaotic production of his 1979 film *Cuba* only made him more distant from Hollywood. When he initially received the *Meteor* script, Connery liked what he read and believed it a unique idea.

However, according to Connery, the original script was heavily rewritten by Neame and Stanley Mann. That, and the difficult production, took its toll on the no-nonsense Scot. Distant from James Bond and in a changing cinematic landscape, the character Dr. Bradley might be more reflective of Connery himself. If Connery was facing a career stall, Malden and Wood were enjoying their own honeymoon phases. Malden had just come off the successful TV series *The Streets of San Francisco* (1972-77) and Wood had been enjoying semi-retirement for most of the decade.

As Dr. Sherwood, Malden plays the role of a frustrated bureaucrat who must deal with endless red tape, government officials, military officers and others filled with doubt and paranoia. At one point, he gets into a heated argument with Washington officials who refuse to believe anything is heading for Earth. When the hostile General

Adlon sees a memo ordering him to help Dr. Dubov, he complains to Sherwood. Sherwood advises him to make endless copies of that memo for endless meetings so when the meteor destroys everything it won't matter.

Wood, in contrast, gives an understated performance, taking advantage of her Russian ancestry and language. According to Neame, the composer Leslie Bricusse recommended her when he heard Neame was seeking an actress who could speak Russian. Wood gives her character a Stalingrad accent, though her family came from Odessa, Ukraine. Largely serving as the translator, she has good chemistry with Connery, despite them not having many scenes to work with - romancing a lady over cold sandwiches and coffee is the most difficult art of all!

Joining Wood as a Russian-speaking character, Brian Keith gives the best performance in the cast. Excluding one colorful phrase he hears from a New York cabbie, he delivers every line in Russian. Dubov is essentially Bradley's doppelganger. In his early scenes in Russia, he complains about the government and is unamused by their calculated approach to everything from the reveal of *Hercules* to the threat they're facing. Keith, enthusiastic behind the language barrier, is consistently amusing to watch.

The remaining actors are fine if underused. Trevor Howard and Henry Fonda are both serviceable as a British astronomical observer and the American President respectively. They don't have much to work with and Howard gives his entire performance from behind a television monitor. He was far more effective alongside Connery as the Detective Superintendent in Sidney Lumet's *The Offence* (1973). Landau as General Adlon, commander of the *Hercules* bunker, is very dismissive of the threat and suspicious of the Russians to the point of paranoia. '80s screen siren Sybil Danning appears briefly too as an ill-fated Alpine skier, a year before she started pushing male moviegoers towards puberty.

"The most monumental film project to be launched In Hollywood in 20 years."

With an estimated budget of $16 million, *Meteor* was the most expensive project AIP ever undertook. Higher in cost than *The Towering Inferno* or *Star Wars*, the goal was to meet the current hunger for disaster fare and thereby become a major hit.

As director, Neame does a serviceable job. Scenes of multiple meetings and frequent talk lend the film a static and straightforward look. His best sequence is the mud flood in the New York subway tunnel, as the *Hercules* team tries to escape. The claustrophobic environment, multiple camera angles and constant flooding resemble Neame's more effective moments in *The Poseidon Adventure*.

The interest with disaster films often lies in seeing how they handle their impending apocalypse. Behind the scenes, AIP fired two effects teams before finally forging

41

ahead with the staff they still had and the remaining budget. The five-mile chunk of Orpheus looks fine - imagine a fish tank rock in space and you're set! The various spacecraft - *Challenger II*, *Hercules* and *Peter the Great* - don't really stand out. Eiji Tsuburaya, for example, made a much better job of photographing such vehicles and planetoids in his collision epic *Gorath* (1962). Towards the finale, the same shots of the missiles in flight are used again and again, indicating a possible lack of available footage.

Incidentally, the meteor itself was a 3-foot, 13-pound plastic foam model designed by effects man Frank Van der Veer. Trying to compete with the latest effects-driven epics, AIP pushed hard on the production but the turnover of effects technicians meant less than 25-50 feet of effects footage was completed per day at one point.[1]

One of the film's most creative shots is during the introduction. We're treated to an Academy aspect ratio (1:37) black-and-white summary of the wonders of space by a narrator. As the camera pans into the asteroid belt, the screen expands outward to 2:35 widescreen and color. This may be a homage to the opening of the 1952 film *This is Cinerama* and the subsequent travelogues presented in that format. Whether it was intentional or not, the shot does speak towards the changes in Hollywood in two different decades. Cinerama - like Cinemascope, VistaVision, Superscope and other widescreen formats - was intended to get moviegoers away from the emerging TV industry. AIP, once a bastion for young adults in the '50s and '60s, was trying to stay relevant, to keep up with changing trends. Arkoff was attempting to bring his self-described formula to moviegoers now watching Luke Skywalker and the neon lights of a Brooklyn discotheque.

Back on Earth, the effects work is pretty mixed. The standout segments are the extended and well-edited Hong Kong tsunami and the impact of a fragment on Manhattan, portions of which would be reused in the 1983 nuclear war TV-movie *The Day After*. Standing out from the pack in complexity was the subway mud flood. After a fragment of the meteor destroys most of Manhattan and damages the bunker of the *Hercules* center, the survivors attempt to escape. The sequence took 21 days to film and cost up to $500,000 according to Neame. The set was something of a nightmare, with tons of slimy mud making it more terrifying than spectacular as a shooting location. Medics with oxygen tanks stood by in the event of actors slipping and falling deep into the mud. Connery himself had to take off two days after breathing in the material used for making the sludge. Malden meanwhile was buried, and Wood was almost hurt by a piece of glass. Remarking on the scene, Connery said: "It was the most frightening set I ever worked on", adding: "the mud looked like chocolate pudding but smelled like crap."

Laurence Rosenthal's score is largely unremarkable. After a strong and melodramatic opening cue, most of his remaining tracks are repetitive, and the triumphant themes for the *Hercules* and *Peter the Great* scenes start to wear thin. There are some decent tracks leading into the destruction of the *Hercules* base, but nothing particularly grand.

"The Americans elected an alchemist for President."

Perhaps the most interesting element of *Meteor* is its message of détente and international cooperation. While much of the screenplay is filled with familiar genre tropes, this element sets the movie apart from its contemporaries.

In the late '70s, it seemed the two global superpower blocs might be nearing a state of peaceful coexistence. The signing of weapons reduction treaties by the Nixon, Ford and Carter administrations implied a safer future was around the corner. To an extent, we see this shift in the film's dynamic between the two teams of scientists. Bradley left NASA when his pet project was transformed into a weapons platform for nuclear missiles. Sherwood as the stymied bureaucrat reflects the worldview of a career scientist who has had to adapt to change, while getting his point across.

The fear of revealing both weapons systems provides the underlying crux of the narrative for the first half. Cold War officials in Washington and Moscow want to avoid this as it compromises the treaties and statements they've signed. Even when Dubov arrives, he remarks that perhaps the People's Republic of China is the real builder of *Peter the Great*. To get past this, Bradley has to ask his counterpart theoretically how he would have designed such a platform and system.

While the American President admits their system exists, the Russians need more convincing. It's not until Dubov telephones his embassy that Russia's UN representative announces the truth about *Peter the Great*. However, the Soviets stress it was designed and built for precisely such a scenario as an impending meteor strike and declare the USSR fully committed to take action that will benefit mankind.

Through the cooperation of these two powers, mankind is able to avoid complete destruction. It's rather ironic that the détente pioneered during the '70s ended two months after this film's release. The Soviet Union sent troops into Afghanistan in December 1979 to prop up their collapsing communist government. The US and her allies began funneling weapons and support to the anti-communist forces in the country. 43 years on, we're still living with the consequences of decisions made in Afghanistan during that period. Events of the last eight years, and the current conflict in Ukraine, mean the chance of any potential cooperation again between both powers is unlikely.

"And there's not a place on Earth to hide."

While principal photography lasted between October 1977 and January 1978, *Meteor*'s release was delayed. With effects reshooting and potential cost overruns, completing the movie seemed like an endless struggle. Finally released in October 1979, it failed to elicit the response Arkoff and AIP expected. Eviscerated by critics, including the self-involved duo of Siskel and Ebert, the movie didn't make its budget back despite an aggressive marketing campaign.

Among these efforts was a comic book by Marvel under the title 'Meteor - Marvel Comics Super Special' with art by Gene Colan. Copies still turn up online and can be purchased for a reasonable price.

Also: An Interview with Hollywood's Leading Special-Effects Man! A Chilling Look at Real-Life Disasters!

The movie itself would do the rounds on TV and home video over the next 20 years. It was formally released on DVD in 2000 by MGM, the owner of AIP's back catalog. This edition featured the original trailer and an insert booklet. Kino Lorber rereleased the movie under their Studio Classics banner on Blu-Ray and DVD in 2014. Unfortunately, all of these discs are out of print. Whether it will be re-released by another company in the future is unknown.

So where does *Meteor* fall? Is it a lost masterpiece? No. Is it worthy of so much criticism? Not really. It's an enjoyable enough film despite its faults. It accomplishes what it sets out to do. It's not the worst of the '70s disaster cycle - for that, see Irwin Allen's *The Swarm*, which showcases what happens when an A-list cast doesn't want to be there.

Arkoff took a risk to bring his company into the next decade, working within a trend started by the majors. Unfortunately, the studio he brought up would close the following year. Its catalog was sold to Filmways, then to Orion Pictures, before landing at MGM towards the end of the '90s. *Meteor* remains an interesting film that marks the close of a fascinating decade of mayhem.

Like Dr. Bradley's original plans for *Hercules*, it was a unique idea, transformed into something beyond the scope previously imagined. The only place it was expected to fall was back to Earth. Which it did... with a bump.

Investigation of a Citizen Above Suspicion

by Allen Rubinstein

How far will a man go to soothe his bruised ego? What if no one can stop him? What if no one tries?

In the end, to whom or what is a man accountable when he wields power in the system? The law? The public? His superiors and colleagues? A belief system? His conscience? The Murder Squad Chief of the Italian police department would like to answer these questions and to do so, he involves himself and those around him in a bizarre parlor game - an ornate manipulation of the institution he commands. This is the wild story that dissects the use of state power in the 1970 film *Investigation of a Citizen Above Suspicion* (*Indagine su un Cittadino al di Sopra di Ogni Sospetto*).

Investigation is the second of four powerful collaborations between director Elio Petri and screenwriter Ugo Pirro, with a ferocious lead performance by Gian Maria Volonté. We follow the protagonist, who is never named, from the day he is promoted from the Murder Squad to head of the Political Division, making him far more powerful and dangerous. He chooses this crossroads, for reasons that become apparent through flashback, to prove for his own satisfaction that he can get away with anything. That he is, indeed, a man above suspicion.

To do so, he dispassionately slashes the neck of his beautiful mistress Augusta Terzi (Florinda Bolkan) with a razor blade. That accomplished, the Chief wanders the crime scene, intentionally leaving evidence of his guilt, and he spends the rest of the film steering the investigation towards himself.

The typical police officers in the film are not shy about

pinning guilt on citizens for little to no reason, but for the Chief, they are willfully blind. Evidence that investigating officers must consider and dismiss includes, but is not limited to:

• Pictures of their boss in the victim's apartment
• His fingerprints on every surface of the victim's apartment
• Bloody footprints from his shoes
• A thread from his tie on the victim's fingernail; the same tie he wears in front of them at the crime scene
• A neighbor eyewitness who encounters him leaving the building
• A suspicious call to a local reporter who recognizes his voice
• A direct confession to a local plumber who he sends to the police to identify him

No matter how clear a trail he leaves of his culpability, no matter how far he escalates this social experiment, his colleagues can't so much as conceive of him as a suspect. It's an outrageous, original and bold conceit of a story, a hypothetical stress test of power.

Petri had worked with Pirro once before, redefining the mafia drama in *We Still Kill the Old Way* (1967). Following the provocation of *Investigation*, they made a sharp union drama in *The Working Class Goes to Heaven* (1971) and the class-conscious crime noir *Property is No Longer a Theft* (1973). Finally, Petri (sans Pirro) offered his take on religious power in *Todo Modo* (*One Way or Another*, 1976). It's a stellar run of political cinema, with a conscious effort to avoid didacticism and let the story pull the audience toward some deeply truthful and disturbing conclusions. In addition to cornering the market on long film titles, *Investigation* was awarded the Best International Feature Oscar in 1971 (as well as Best Film and Best Actor at the Italian movie awards), and Petri became an international force in the waning days of Italian supremacy over the European film scene.

In his position among the elite of Italian 'art cinema', Petri uneasily walked the tightrope between mainstream/genre film production and radical leftist filmmaking. Following on the models of Costa Gavras' *Z* (1969 - another Oscar winner), Peter Watkins' *The War Game* (1966) and *The Gladiators* (1969), and to a lesser extent Lindsey Anderson's *If....* (1968), their dedication to peeling back the layers of a corrupt society launched toward an engaged, politicized young audience. These directors coated radical critique in established genre tropes and familiar story structure. They communicated ideas by making politics exciting and entertaining to watch, earning the critique of some who saw the very nature of traditional forms, to say nothing of working within conservative financing channels, as inherently compromising.

While it might be silly to take to task a political film with the nerve to tell a thrilling, coherent story, there's something to this. Petri and his peers have spoken often of the challenges of making movies that explicitly question the values of the wealthy and powerful while using the money of the wealthy and powerful to ensure the film gets made. They're hemmed between pressure to go mainstream while getting the side-eye from their film's natural audience for not being sufficiently revolutionary. With Hollywood's trendy, less radical string of '70s paranoid thrillers on one side and Jean-Luc Godard's frankly non-commercial Marxist tracks on the other (plus some of the more searing documentaries of the time), Petri and his colleagues occupied some uneasy film real estate - trying to satisfy many but pleasing few.

However one may regard different strains of political cinema, their injection into the historical conversation is undeniable. More than its accolades, *Investigation of a Citizen Above Suspicion* made its mark in Italy in light of recent local events. Student and worker uprisings had been escalating in number and violence for several years at the start of a decade of social unrest that became known as "the years of lead". Three months before the picture's first screenings in Italy, a bomb blew apart Milan's Piazza Fortuna killing seventeen people and wounding 88 others. Leftist groups and leaders were rounded up in a manner similar to a key sequence in the film, upon which anarchist **Giuseppe Pinelli** "accidentally fell" from a fourth-story window, killing him.

Investigation had wrapped shooting weeks before this happened but was viewed as representing them anyway. It was hard to watch the newly released picture and

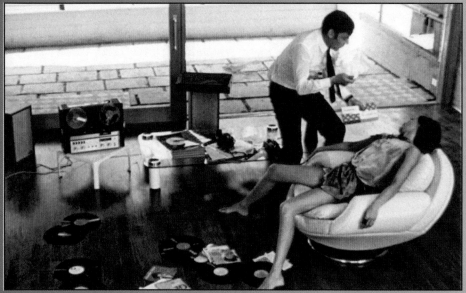

not think it was about the recent controversy. Some thought the film's protagonist was a direct stand-in for Commissioner **Luigi Calabresi who oversaw the fatal interrogation.** Anger and distrust with Italian authorities was at an all-time high, and only fear of reprisals kept Petri's film from being censored or pulled entirely. Stories had long circulated about law enforcement infiltrating, instigating and even funding terrorist activity as a pretense for torturing and jailing subversives. The US was hardly the only nation working to delegitimize counterculture social movements, curtailing their success as political organizers and promoters of anti-authoritarian ideology.

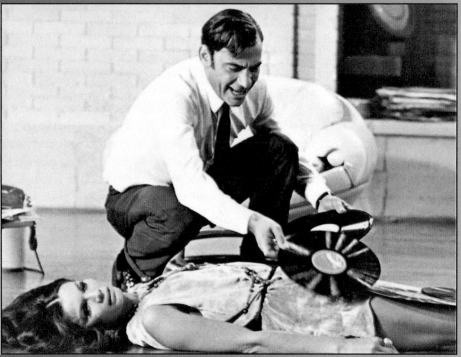

Of course it was prescient. Of course, Elio Petri would know and understand all of this. This isn't some studio hack pulling a pile of Nehru jackets and tie-dye T-shirts out of wardrobe for a team of extras; he and Pirro were committed leftists who knew their milieu. *Investigation* foresaw The Pentagon Papers, Watergate, Iran-Contra and the entire Trump Administration. *Investigation of a Citizen Above Suspicion* predicted the notorious window-dropping incident because authoritarians committing violence on their opposition is predictable.

Which brings us back to the Chief of the Murder Squad. The Chief starts the film at the peak of his political power. He can spy on, arrest, detain and interrogate any person he deems culpable for crimes real or imagined. He has carte blanche from his superiors, and the other functionaries of Italian law enforcement either worship him or cower before him or both.

Just the fact that he felt not only the necessity but the freedom to engage in this exercise is mind-boggling. He puts at risk his career, his name, his freedom - everything to prove a point to no person besides himself. He dares the police to even imagine that the man they pursue is someone in their midst, someone in a position of authority, someone they know, respect and admire, someone aligned with their politics, goals and world view.

The man carries that Trumpian combination of rock-hard public certainty with private feet of clay, yet for all the Chief's hidden doubts and insecurities, none relate to his institutional mission - to crush the left in all its forms. It's what drives him. Gian Maria Volonté's portrayal makes for a propulsive ride. He is in perpetual motion throughout the runtime, his mind planning and scheming like a scalpel and his jaw set in determination. The Chief's fiery speech at the film's midpoint makes it clear that to the new Political Division Chief, subversive thought is as prosecutable as murder, no matter the statutes. "Every criminal can turn out to be a subversive. Every subversive can turn out to be a criminal. In the city we have become accustomed to, subversives and criminals have already laid down their web which we have to destroy. What difference is there between a gang of robbers who attack a bank and organized institutionalized and legalised subversion? None."

Not once does he posit what the onus of labor strikes or radical newspapers might pose to the public at large (nor homosexuality, put forward as evidence of criminality and perversion numerous times). The danger is exclusively to the power structure. "The use of freedom is a threat to traditional powers, to the authorities. The use of freedom which tends to make every citizen a judge, that prevents us from carrying out our sacred duties. We are guarding the law that we want to remain unchanged, etched in time."

That all the events of the film contradict his fealty to law is of no concern. There is an enemy and he gathers the tools to destroy them. Meanwhile, the Chief's animosity toward union organizing is plain convenience. He threatens to report an intelligence officer who asks for a raise, and bellows to have the coffee machine removed because it encourages idle conversation. Indeed, he wants to start

GIAN MARIA VOLONTÉ · FLORINDA BOLKAN · SALVO RANDONE

"INVESTIGATION OF A CITIZEN above suspicion"

Directed by Elio Petri
Produced by Marina Cicogna Daniele Senatore
Screenplay by Elio Petri Ugo Pirro
Starring Gian Maria Volonté Florinda Bolkan
Music by Ennio Morricone
Cinematography Luigi Kuveiller
Edited by Ruggero Mastroianni   TECHNICOLOR

investigating the agents of the murder squad he was just promoted out of.

The great thing about political fiction is that it can take what is disguised behind myth or ideology and expose it to light. I emerged from my first screening of *Investigation* thinking: "Boy, the Italians sure know their fascists." From Bertolluci's *The Conformist* (1970) to Pasolini's *Salo: or the 120 Days of Sodom* (1975) or even historical films like *Sacco e Vanzetti* (Guilianon Montaldo, 1971) and the *Assassination of Matteoti* (Florestano Vancini, 1973), their totalitarian monsters are not merely stand-ins for any generic moustache twirler, but a specific set of proclivities, neuroses and red flags it would be wise for victims under the boot to be familiar with and know how to interpret. Petri's film wants to render the strategies and shoddy rhetoric of the right visible to the audience.

Investigation spells out what makes fascists tick. Much of that work is done in flashback with Bolkan's Augusta Tenzi and her explicit conversations with her hand-picked power lover. The future murder victim is a shit-stirrer of Italian proportions - a mercurial, super-model-gorgeous provocateur with a taste for powerful men and a talent for savaging her partners' ugliest insecurities. Her character is tailor-made to instigate the events of the film single-handedly, unknowingly inspiring her own death.

It's here that Petri gets to touch on the psycho-sexual aspect of the Fascist mindset that was the basis of the entirety of Pasolini's *Salo*. Much is made of Augusta never wearing or owning undergarments, something related more than once to Gabrielle D'Annunzio, a writer in the Decadent movement who rivalled Mussolini as the father of Italian fascism. Augusta and the Chief's foreplay consists of re-enacting and photographing murder scenes while he describes them to her in grisly detail. Every authoritarian instinct of the Chief is a turn-on for Augusta. She goads him to run a red light in full view of a traffic cop and gleefully commands: "Be mean to him" as they are pulled over, not out of cruelty or sadism, but to demonstrate that he will not be touched by behavior that would doom any ordinary citizen.

In a moment of relaxed boredom, Augusta insists that the Chief interrogate her as her would a murder suspect, and while slapping and manhandling her, he expounds a shorthand instruction manual for extracting confessions from the guilty and innocent.

"[Remember] the most shameful images of your life. I can find out everything about you because the state lets me find out everything about everyone. Think I know everything, so you'll start feeling guilty. Confess everything, your weaknesses, your minor daily embarrassments. Only in doing so will you obtain my forgiveness and my protection."

"I get it. You're treating me like a child."

"We all go back to children when faced with someone who represents power and authority. All laws; the known laws and the unknown laws. And I become the father, the unchallengeable model. My face becomes that of God of conscience. It's just an act to touch deep chords, secret emotions." He then expands his analysis to include any official position of power. "This is what the authorities base themselves on: university professors, party leaders, tax collectors, station masters." The Chief then feeds her a chocolate and covers her with flowers, making himself the arbiter of reward and punishment. It's these passages that elevate Petri's film above any ordinary police procedural or thriller as an essential text for anyone living under an oppressive government.

In that same scene, Augusta turns the tables on him. "You're like a kid. More than any other man I've known." It's a curious line, given the dialogue that precedes it, in its self-awareness and cold calculation. If she's not simply reflecting his enthusiastic embrace of his role, then she's seeing his overwhelming need to know, control and dominate. He does not take it well. "You shouldn't have said that," he responds. "The others are kids. Do you understand that?"

She spends the better part of her screen time belittling the Chief in moods both playful and angry. The following is part of her initial *seduction* technique, a series of uninvited phone calls she decides to make after seeing him on the news: "Try to lose weight. You always wear dark clothes. You're always in mourning. Don't get your hopes up. I don't find you attractive. You're too average-Italian. You have too much hair. It's clear you sweat a lot. I bet you smell like shoe polish, right? Like all cops."

Later, once they're involved, she continues. "You wear short socks like a priest... You smell like a cell, like an archive, like a security room. Get the authorities to buy you a deodorant." Augusta then sits on his lap and cuts his tie off with scissors.

He responds: "I could kill you with my bare hands."

Later comes her coup de grace: "You are a child, and you make love like a child. Maybe you still wet the bed. You're a nobody. You're sexually incompetent," to which he responds by indeed having a small tantrum like he's being scolded by mommy.

And then she's gone. She plants the seed of an idea for plotting some great crime he can get away with, injures his masculinity, and is dispatched to become a lurid news item and some empty accusations that a neighbor did it or her jealous ex-husband. Her only legacy is a burning need in the former Murder Squad Chief to establish once and for all that his mission to snuff out independent thought among the public is far more important than some attractive woman with a slit throat.

The protagonist of *Investigation of a Citizen Above Suspicion* is clearly a fanatic, and his actions in the film are unhinged. None of that matters, though, to those above him. We're introduced early on to the Police Commissioner the Chief reports to, who determines the source and level of his department's resources. Ensconced in an office with archaeological relics and Catholic paintings, the Commissioner can blithely sanction inappropriate relationships with informants, give officers permission to hide evidence

and approve human rights abuses. He has the unmistakable air of a mafia don and appears at the end of the film to simply absolve the protagonist with full knowledge of what he's done.

What the Chief discovers is that the extent to which he is above suspicion depends on the will of those more powerful than himself. He is untouchable because he is useful and loyal. He bows his head to the Commissioner in the film's final shot, secure that he will faithfully pursue the will and agenda of those who ensure him a place above suspicion, above consequences. The activists, plumbers and criminals of the street are chattel. The Chief is as much a servant to power as an arbiter of it.

Petri's film ends with a quote from Franz Kafka: "Whatever he may seem to us, he is yet a servant of the law. That is, he belongs to the law, and as such is set beyond human judgement." In this case, it refers to the law and nature of the powerful, what they need and want, and who is protected by them, not by any mere legal matters enshrined in books and paper. The film that Elio Petri and Ugo Pirro made is a chilling and important document to that fact.

Brian J. Robb looks at the 1970s director collectives BBS Productions and The Directors Company that were built around 'star name' directors and rewrote the Hollywood rules...

Hollywood in the early '70s saw new power come into the hands of film directors. The efficient, factory-like studio production system that had served the Hollywood studios so well since the '30s had more-or-less collapsed during the '60s. By the end of that decade, what came to be known as the 'American New Wave' (named after the French nouvelle vague or 'new wave' of the '60s) put the director foremost in the creation of feature films, as the 'author' or auteur behind the work, relegating the once all-powerful producer to a second-tier figure (and confirming the insignificance of screenwriters in the hierarchy of power). The 'author' of movies in this 'New Hollywood' was not the studio, not the producer, nor the screenwriter, but the director.

Given that, it stands to reason that the best of these directors would make moves to consolidate their new-found power. Independent productions had always existed outside the mainstream studio system, but they had grown in stature since the '50s when actors began to break away from their restrictive studio contracts and establish their own production companies. Likewise, in the late '60s and early '70s directors followed suit with

several teaming up to form their own independent production entities.

The two most prominent were the short-lived BBS Productions and The Directors Company. Both were idealistic operations reflecting their times, but like so many of the 'baby boomer' efforts of the '60s, both ultimately failed in their aims, although they did have a lasting (not necessarily positive) effect on Hollywood. The low-key, naturalistic films these companies produced were reactions against the kind of overblown flops that came during the decline of the studio system - like *Cleopatra* (1963), *Doctor Doolittle* (1967), and *Star!* (1968) - as much as they were an attempt to find a new language for American movies through the '70s.

Directors to the Fore

The first of these director-led co-operatives of the early '70s was BBS

Productions. It began life in the '60s as Raybert Productions, a company formed by director Bob Rafelson and producer Bert Schneider (the company title came from putting their names together 'Ra(y)' and 'Bert'). Their main focus in the mid '60s was on the television series *The Monkees*, which featured a manufactured, Beatles-like American foursome in a series of wacky adventures modelled after The Beatles movies of the '60s, *A Hard Day's Night* (1964) and *Help!* (1965), directed in London by American Richard Lester. *The Monkees* ran for two seasons to 1968, making stars of

David Jones, Micky Dolenz, Michael Nesmith and Peter Tork. Schneider and Rafelson produced the show through Raybert Productions for Screen Gems and made a lot of money doing so.

Rafelson made his feature film directorial debut with The Monkees' movie *Head* (1968), for which he co-wrote the script with young actor Jack Nicholson. That in turn led to the ground-breaking counter-culture classic road movie *Easy Rider* (1969), a co-production between Raybert and co-writer and star Peter Fonda's company Pando Company Inc. Nicholson co-starred with Fonda and nominal director Dennis Hopper (although it was more of a communal effort). Produced for well under $500,000, *Easy Rider* met with critical acclaim and stunning box office success, scoring worldwide takings of around $60 million. It effectively captured the last gasp of '60s idealism, before the cultural 'hangover' of the '70s hit.

After the collapse of The Monkees - the short-lived vogue for the band soon petered out and *Head* was a troubled production - Rafelson moved on to direct *Five Easy Pieces* (1970), featuring Nicholson as a rootless oil worker (once a young piano prodigy) who travels with his girlfriend (Karen Black) to visit his dying father. A critical hit, *Five Easy Pieces* was seen as the film that brought the European alienation of the likes of Michelangelo Antonioni to American film (Nicholson would later feature in Antonioni's *The Passenger*, 1975). Rafelson's *Five Easy Pieces* was nominated for four Oscars, including Best Picture, Best Actor for Nicholson, Best Supporting Actor for Black and Best Original Screenplay (Rafelson and Carole Eastman), but won none.

In the wake of *Five Easy Pieces*, Raybert transformed into BBS Productions with the addition of Steve Blauner (the former manager of Bobby Darin, who shared Rafelson's television background, and a childhood friend of Schneider's). Taking the initials of the three principals, the company became BBS Productions. Their aim was to combine the sensibility of serious European filmmaking with the '60s values of people like Hopper and Nicholson, and they had their share of the funds from *Easy Rider* to back them. In its brief existence, BBS would produce just five further films, but it provided a home for many graduates from cult exploitation filmmaking outfit American International Pictures (AIP), where both Nicholson and Hopper got their starts.

Five Easy Pieces had set the tone, one that would continue to inform each of the BBS productions that reached the screen: *Drive, He Said* (1971), *The Last Picture Show* (1971), *A Safe Place* (1971), *The King of Marvin Gardens* (1972) and the Vietnam war-focused documentary *Hearts and Minds* (1974). Those behind BBS Productions were determined to work outside the Hollywood establishment, bringing to the screen a new approach to naturalism rather than the studio-created 'heightened realism' that had begun, through the '60s and into the '70s, to look increasingly artificial. Although most of those involved were in their thirties, their aim was to reflect the concerns of America's youth as they navigated their way into adulthood.

There was a new freedom inherent in the director-led projects in early '70s American cinema; freedom from the restrictions of the studios, freedom from the demands

COLUMBIA PICTURES Presents a BBS Production

JACK NICHOLSON

FIVE EASY PIECES

KAREN BLACK and SUSAN ANSPACH

Screenplay by ADRIEN JOYCE

Story by BOB RAFELSON and ADRIEN JOYCE

Produced by BOB RAFELSON and RICHARD WECHSLER

Executive Producer BERT SCHNEIDER • Directed by BOB RAFELSON

COLOR R C

and indulgences of 'star' names, and a new physical freedom allowed by new, more lightweight cameras and equipment that allowed for much of films like *Easy Rider* and *Five Easy Pieces* to be shot on the fly in genuine cross-country odysseys. Just as those involved in the politics of the Richard Nixon era were asking where America might go next, so those exploiting this new-found creative freedom were asking themselves the vital question: where could American cinema go next?

It's Who You Know!

Despite these ambitions, BBS still relied upon the 'old' Hollywood for its distribution, affiliating with Columbia, once the fiefdom of the formidable movie mogul Harry Cohn. The association came about through a family connection: Bert Schneider's father Abe Schneider had begun at the studio as an office boy but had

succeeded Cohn as President of the entire company in 1958. Through his sponsorship of BBS Productions, the senior Schneider pioneered the idea of Hollywood studios working closely with independent outfits, taking in Stanley Kramer's independent company and Hecht-Hill-Lancaster, an independent vehicle for Burt Lancaster that led to *Birdman of Alcatraz* (1962). In supporting BBS, Abe Schneider made sure that an old Hollywood studio like Columbia (always, futilely, in search of a defining identity or stylistic feature) had at least one eye on the future of film as it would unfold through the '70s.

A six-picture deal (including *Five Easy Pieces*) was worked out between Columbia and BBS, with a theatrical release guaranteed for each film while the right of 'final cut' and complete creative control remained with the filmmakers. Each film would have a budget of up to $1 million (at

least twice that of *Easy Rider*) and any budget overruns would have to be covered by the producers - essentially BBS - themselves.

Schneider explained (in 'Hollywood Films of the Seventies: Sex, Drugs, Violence, Rock 'n' Roll & Politics') the unique approach BBS took to making movies: "We do not care what the story content of a film is, who the stars are, or if there are stars involved. We are concerned only with who is making the film. If his energy and personality project something unique, he is given the freedom and help to express himself." This was entirely contradictory to the way the Hollywood studios usually operated, where the producer made just about all the creative decisions, with writers and directors treated as simply necessary cogs in the filmmaking machine, needed to create the final product but unimportant in themselves.

Easy Rider and *Five Easy Pieces* set the template for BBS Productions to follow. Their next five films of the '70s both matched and expanded the ambitions of the filmmakers, offering further opportunities to the likes of Rafelson and Nicholson while broadening out their talent pool to include other like-minded directors such as Peter Bogdanovich (*The Last Picture Show*) and Henry Jaglom (*A Safe Place*). The documentary *Hearts and Minds* was a last-gasp attempt to broaden the range of BBS Productions, just before the final curtain fell on the operation.

Give Peace a Chance

In *Drive, He Said*, director and co-writer Jack Nicholson indulged himself in the tale of ennui on a college campus. Capturing the free-for-all sexual zeitgeist of the early '70s and the increasingly strident anti-Vietnam war sentiment of the nation's youth, *Drive, He Said* (the title comes from a poem) met a stormy reception when screened at Cannes. The movie ran head-on into

COLUMBIA PICTURES
Presents
A BBS PRODUCTION

DRIVE, HE SAID

Directed by
JACK NICHOLSON

AN OFFICIAL
UNITED STATES ENTRY
CANNES
FILM FESTIVAL

starring
WILLIAM TEPPER · KAREN BLACK · MICHAEL MARGOTTA · BRUCE DERN
ROBERT TOWNE · HENRY JAGLOM · MIKE WARREN   Screenplay by Jeremy Larner
and Jack Nicholson · Produced by Steve Blauner and Jack Nicholson
Executive Producer Bert Schneider

a young women (Weld) who lives in a fantasy world and refuses to grow up thanks to a fear of adulthood. Jaglom (who'd helped to edit *Easy Rider*) was an idiosyncratic filmmaker who liked to simply let the camera run while his cast went through their paces. He produced in excess of 50 hours of footage which he culled down to carve out the 94-minute finished film - it was the most experimental of BBS's movies. Welles featured as a stage magician (what else?) who may or may not be an imaginary figure only seen by Weld's disturbed (and ultimately doomed) character (Jaglom would appear in Welles' unfinished *The Other Side of the Wind*). Jaglom's working methods drew

MICHEL SEYDOUX présente :

TUESDAY WELD · ORSON WELLES
JACK NICHOLSON

A SAFE PLACE

UN COIN TRANQUILLE

un film de
HENRY JAGLOM

PHIL PROCTOR · GWEN WELLES
A BBS PICTURE · PRODUCTEUR EXÉCUTIF BERT SCHNEIDER · DISTRIBUTION CAMERA ONE

a censorship controversy thanks to a basketball locker-room sequence featuring full-frontal male nudity (a big 'no-no' at the time, and still less than commonplace today). Female sexuality was to the fore, also, as Karen Black's Olive was depicted experiencing an orgasm (something seen in European cinema as far back as Hedy Lamarr's notorious scene in 1933's *Extase/Ecstasy*). Critic Roger Ebert dubbed Nicholson's debut film "disorganized but occasionally brilliant."

Jaglom's *A Safe Place* was a different type of film entirely. Nicholson turned up here again, co-starring with then 27-year-old Tuesday Weld and Orson Welles in a tale of upon those pioneered in the late '50s and through the '60s by John Cassavetes, structured improvisation in the service of capturing 'truth'. Like *Drive, He Said*, *A Safe Place* was a box office flop which grew in critical estimation over the decades that followed; it was largely regarded as 'pretentious' at the time but was re-evaluated as part of later reconsiderations of the BBS project.

Certainly the most impactful of the BBS movies was Peter Bogdanovich's debut *The Last Picture Show*, which launched his career and that of Jeff Bridges. The most successful of the BBS output, *The Last Picture Show* - an elegiac look back at small town America - scored eight Oscar nominations, winning two for Ben Johnson as Best Supporting Actor (Bridges was nominated in the same category) and Cloris Leachman as Best Supporting Actress. Bogdanovich would dine out on the success of his debut picture for the rest of his incredibly variable career, but of all the new directors to emerge through the BBS project, he was probably the most successful.

King of the Cinema

Rafelson himself returned to the director's chair for what would be BBS's final dramatic film, *The King of Marvin Gardens*. Nicholson again starred (this pivotal BBS figure here cast against type as an introvert), alongside *Drive, He Said*'s Bruce Dern (as Nicholson's brother) and Ellen Burstyn in the tale of a get-rich-quick-scheme that (naturally) doesn't pay off in the anticipated way. Perhaps drawing upon Jaglom's approach in *A Safe Place*, Rafelson

"A superb metaphor for what has often been called 'The American Dream'! The performances are fabulous!"
—ARTHUR KNIGHT
Saturday Review

Columbia Pictures presents a BBS Production

The King of Marvin Gardens Ⓜ

Jack Nicholson   Bruce Dern
Ellen Burstyn

with Julia Anne Robinson · Benjamin (Scatman) Crothers
Screenplay by Jacob Brackman · Original Story by
Bob Rafelson and Jacob Brackman · Executive Producer Steve Blauner
Produced and Directed by Bob Rafelson   COLOR

went beyond BBS's declared interest in a new 'naturalism' by including several surreal scenes. The film was shot on location in the winter off-season in Atlantic City before much of the historical centre was redeveloped. This was a film that reached beyond the filmmakers' capabilities in attempting to infuse the 'every day' reality of an increasingly run-down America with a kind of European poetic realism. Critic Roger Ebert felt the picture took "a lot of chances", scoring "on about sixty percent of them." Downbeat and desolate, *The King of Marvin Gardens* was as close as BBS ever came to capturing the sense of hopelessness that pervaded Nixon's America. With *The King of Marvin Gardens*, BBS reached the end of the road.

Politics - whether of the personal, sexual or party kind - was often at the centre of BBS's films, even if it was often disguised by the surface-level drama unfolding on screen. The radical politics of the period infiltrated the films and had a real-life effect on the filmmakers. Rafelson told Peter Biskind (in 'Easy Riders, Raging Bulls') that "people were getting shot in the [BBS] building because of the politics, the Black Panther stuff, busts and cops and God knows what. I didn't know who was in that building. None of them could pay... I felt I was burned out." As BBS entered its final days, Rafelson declared "a joyous closing of the door. We decided to quit while we were ahead."

The final production was completely different: a documentary aiming to capture a sense of the time and place in which it was made. *Hearts and Minds* nailed BBS's colours to the wall in its outright opposition to the war in Vietnam. Directed by Peter Davis (who made the controversial 1971 *CBS Reports* documentary *The Selling of the Pentagon*, that examined increasing taxpayers funding of the military-industrial complex), the film explored the origins of the Vietnam war and how it was conducted by the American forces. The title came from the government's declared 'hearts and minds' strategy to persuade the public to support the war, a strategy that was manifestly failing.

During post-production, there was a change of executives at Columbia (Abe Schneider left the board in 1975) that saw the studio attempt to cut all ties with BBS, especially over the controversial Vietnam documentary. The documentary played at Cannes, where the reception was much more positive than that afforded Nicholson's *Drive, He Said* (which had also engaged critically with US militarism). Columbia sold the movie back to BBS for $1

million and it was released by Jaglom through a special deal with Warner Bros. for a single week in LA in order to qualify for the Oscars. This proved to be a prescient decision, as *Hearts and Minds* won that year's Oscar for Best Documentary, a fitting capstone to the overall BBS project.

The Vietnam war ended (no 'winner' could realistically be declared) in April 1975, with *Hearts and Minds* still on general release. It was fitting in a way that the war that had provided the anti-establishment subtext to many of BBS's innovative movies should end at the same time as the company itself being wound up. The collapse of Columbia Pictures into bankruptcy in the early '70s eventually caught up with BBS Productions. In the absence of Abe Schneider as a sponsor, the studio dropped BBS in favour of concentrating on solving its own financial troubles.

Bob Rafelson would go on to enjoy a strong career through the '70s, taking in the likes of *Stay Hungry* (1976), featuring Jeff Bridges, and into the '80s with noir remake *The Postman Always Rings Twice* (1981) and *Black Widow* (1987); he died in July 2022, aged 89. Henry Jaglom carved out his own idiosyncratic career with films like *Tracks* (1976), starring Dennis Hopper, and is still around aged 84. Peter Bogdanovich also died in 2022, aged 82, after coming to personify the 'New Hollywood' with the likes of *What's Up, Doc?* (1972), *Paper Moon* (1973) and *Nickelodeon* (1976).

It was rather fitting that BBS should provide a home for so many former AIP filmmakers and actors (and despite

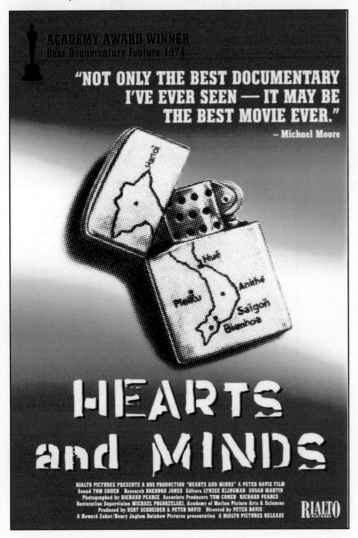

the focus on directors, BBS seemed particularly fixated on a handful of specific actors), like Bogdanovich (*Targets*, 1968), Karen Black, Jack Nicholson, Henry Jaglom and Bruce Dern, as well as the likes of cinematographer László Kovács and screenwriter Carole Eastman. The spirit of anarchy and experimentation of AIP's exploitation pictures (many under the stewardship of Roger Corman) laid the groundwork for the American new wave so radically embodied by BBS.

Idealists Unite!

Peter Bogdanovich was the link between BBS Productions and The Directors Company, an organisation that very much followed in the creative footsteps of Rafelson and company. The Directors Company

grew out of the success that Francis Ford Coppola enjoyed with *The Godfather* in 1972. Paramount and producer Robert Evans were keen to keep a reluctant Coppola attached to the planned sequel, and recognising the newly emerging auteurist tendency in American cinema (which put the director's vision first), they knew they'd have to make any deal very attractive.

Coppola always prized his independence, even as he entered the studio system during its dying days with *The Rain People* in 1969. His Oscar-winning success (Best Picture, Best Actor, Best Adapted Screenplay) with *The Godfather* (a project he'd initially dismissed) and his reluctant commitment to *The Godfather Part II* (1974) gave Coppola the clout to make his passion project, *The Conversation* (1974) - the first of the projects produced under The Directors Company banner.

To tie Coppola in more deeply with Paramount, the studio agreed to finance this grouping of three then-prominent directors: Coppola, Bogdanovich (off the back of his BBS production *The Last Picture Show*), and William Friedkin (who'd scored five Oscars - including Best Picture, Best Director, and Best Adapted Screenplay - for *The French*

Connection, 1971). They were all hot properties, and while individually they could negotiate great deals with studios hungry for auteurist products, they felt that together they would stand a better chance of retaining final cut and creative control. According to Friedkin (in his memoir 'The Friedkin Connection') the idea for what became The Directors Company originated with Charles Bluhdorn, chairman of Gulf and Western, the then owners of Paramount. The problem was that the highly remunerative deal that

Bluhdorn struck with the talent he wanted connected with the studio was completed without the support of Paramount's President Frank Yablans, who was against giving 'mere filmmakers' such extraordinary power and rewards. The seeds of the downfall of The Directors Company were sown in its very creation.

The unprecedented deal was done in 1972, committing the trio of directors to make three films, with each costing no more than $3 million (a medium budget at the time). The initial plan was for Coppola to make *The Conversation*, a script he'd long nurtured (although neither Bogdanovich nor Friedkin were keen for this to be the first film from the group), with Bogdanovich making his period piece *Paper Moon*, and Friedkin planning on shooting *The Bunker Hill Boys*. A more ambitious plan involved the making of up to 12 pictures with a possible move into television. The company was controlled by a board of directors made up of the three movie directors and three executives from Paramount who would give each project the green light.

The most enthusiastic of the three was Bogdanovich, who'd experienced something of a similar set-up with BBS Productions. For Coppola, The Directors Company was merely a vehicle to get Paramount to fund *The Conversation* and Friedkin was the most reluctant of the trio to throw his lot in on a collective endeavour, but Bogdanovich was genuinely enthused by the set-up.

"I thought it was a great idea'" he told the 'Hollywood Reporter' in a retrospective interview in 2013. "The money we could make was limited to a certain amount, which I thought was perfectly good, but Friedkin felt he wanted more money, and more money for the budget. Our deal was, we could make any picture we wanted, as long as it was three million or under, which was a lot of money in those days. We could also produce a movie for someone else if it wasn't more than $1.5 million. We didn't even have to show them a script! It was a great deal, and I wish I could get one like it again. That kind of freedom is worth gold, I think."

Paramount's Peter Bart supervised the independent off-shoot (Bart followed his career as a studio executive with a lengthy period

as editor-in-chief of film industry newspaper 'Variety'). He backed Bogdanovich, who quickly and efficiently made Depression-set comedy-drama *Paper Moon*, starring Ryan O'Neal, his daughter Tatum O'Neal and Madeline Kahn. A critical and commercial success, it narrowly beat Coppola's *The Conversation* into release. Coppola's movie was a huge critical hit, but less commercially successful than *Paper Moon*, although it still did well enough. While Friedkin dragged his feet, Bogdanovich quickly

moved onto a new project for The Directors Company, the ill-fated *Daisy Miller* (1974).

Based on the Henry James novel, the period film featured Bogdanovich's then-girlfriend Cybill Shepherd in the title role, a part she was unsuited for. The film was a flop, and one that Bogdanovich came to regret making. "I knew when we were making it that it wasn't commercial," he admitted, while also recognising that his partners in The Directors Company were not keen on the project either. "They thought it was a kind of vanity production to show Cybill off." In his memoir, Friedkin recalled: "I told Peter he shouldn't make [*Daisy Miller*] for our company. We had promised Bluhdorn "commercial" films." Friedkin suspected that Yablans was encouraging Bogdanovich behind the scenes in the hope that the failure of *Daisy Miller* would lead to the end of The Directors Company.

The Force Isn't with Them

The commercial nous of the principals in The Directors Company appears to have been a little suspect in any event. Friedkin recalled that Coppola had brought them the script of *Star Wars* by George Lucas and they had the opportunity to make the film, but declined as neither Friedkin nor Bogdanovich were keen on it! Bogdanovich increasingly came to regard The Directors Company as a vehicle through which he could help his 'old Hollywood' director friends return to work, including Orson Welles and King Vidor. Bogdanovich had lobbied Paramount to pick up Welles' *The Other Side of the Wind* in 1973, to no avail. Friedkin's announced *The Bunker Hill Boys* vanished without trace and he never made a film for The Directors Company.

It was largely Friedkin's attitude that led to the end of The Directors Company. As well as not contributing a film of his own, he disparaged the efforts of the others. He liked *Paper Moon* well enough, but thought *Daisy Miller* was a mistake, and he had a very poor opinion of Coppola's *The Conversation*, regarding it as a remake of 1966's *Blow-Up*. The tensions between the three creatives and the problems with Paramount over what films to make combined to cause The Directors Company to implode after the release of just three films, two of them directed by Bogdanovich.

Looking back, in a 2004 interview with Peter Bart at 'Variety', Friedkin said: "The chief problem with The Directors Company... was that it was never really a company. The three filmmakers involved in its founding ... relished the basic precepts of the enterprise, but, as true 1970s mavericks, resisted serious involvement in its operation. Which was a shame because, had the company survived, these three (and other) filmmakers had much to gain from it. All three of the founding filmmakers went on to display rather arcane choices in material for their next films. All could have benefited from a collegial give

and take with their peers. Further, the basic structure of the company was valid, perhaps ahead of its time. It made sense for a studio to assign a portion of its filmmaking programme to directors who would function with a high degree of autonomy."

Friedkin, however, turned his back on The Directors Company long before any of this utopian approach could come to fruition. Instead, he focused on his own project, 1973's *The Exorcist*, and never looked back. Coppola went on to make *The Godfather Part II* and moved between his own independent productions and 'for hire' work for the studios for the rest of his career. Bogdanovich, likewise, kept moving forward, making the most of any filmmaking opportunities afforded him.

Filmmakers controlling their own films has been a utopian project in Hollywood ever since United Artists was established in 1919 by Charlie Chaplin, Mary Pickford, Douglas Fairbanks and D. W. Griffith, a development famously greeted by producer Richard Rowland with the pronouncement that "the lunatics have taken over the asylum!" The asylum of Hollywood continued to be assailed by filmmaking 'lunatics' in the decades that followed.

Perhaps the greatest beneficiaries of the 'New Hollywood' of the '70s were Francis Ford Coppola and George Lucas, two directors who largely kept away from these collective endeavours - Coppola was only really part of The Directors Company due to his dealings with Paramount over *The Conversation* and *The Godfather Part II*. He'd long wanted to make a go of it on his own through his company American Zoetrope, which he originally envisaged as a collective filmmaking effort that would offer opportunities to up-and-coming directors.

Similarly, Lucas (who made *THX 1138* for American Zoetrope) found himself having to go it alone under his Lucasfilm banner, coming to rely on 20th Century Fox to finance 1977's *Star Wars* (which along with Spielberg's *Jaws* ushered in the high concept blockbuster era). His success saw Lucas create Skywalker Ranch, a Northern Californian post-production facility encompassing Skywalker Sound and special effects house Industrial Light & Magic (based at The Presidio in nearby San Francisco). Lucasfilm - which gave birth to Pixar - was an independent entity producing the Star Wars and Indiana Jones films (among others) until 2012, when Lucas sold out to Disney.

Ironically, the co-operative endeavours of the likes of BBS Productions and The Directors Company in the 1970s that put the director above all other movie creatives gave rise to the success of the filmmakers who would usher in the 'high concept' blockbuster filmmaking era of the '80s, a time completely antithetical to the aims and ambitions of the likes of Rafelson, Schneider, Jaglom, Bogdanovich and Friedkin.

PRIME CUT
PRIME CINEMA

by James Lecky

The gangster film has always been a Hollywood staple, going back at least as far as Mervyn LeRoy's *Little Caesar* (1931), William A. Wellman's *The Public Enemy* (1931) and Howard Hawks' *Scarface* (1932). Distinct from close cousins like the detective film or the thriller, the gangster film as a sub-genre specifically focuses on career criminals.

Largely consigned to fertile B-movie territory (but occasionally emerging into the mainstream), gangster films came into their own thanks to the success of Arthur Penn's *Bonnie and Clyde* (1967) and, perhaps more importantly, Francis Ford Coppola's *The Godfather* (1972). Both were stylishly shot, impeccably performed and featured unrepentant outlaws as protagonists.

Prior to *Bonnie and Clyde*, American crime films had been predominantly urban, as though crime itself was a predominantly urban phenomenon. Film noir generally took place against a concrete landscape, but Penn's film opened up the landscape.

In the early '70s, there were a particular group of movies that might be referred to collectively as "rural crime" entries - Sam Peckinpah's *The Getaway* (1972), Terrence Malick's *Badlands* (1973), John Milius' *Dillinger* (1973), Michael Cimino's *Thunderbolt and Lightfoot* (1974), John Hough's *Dirty Mary, Crazy Larry* (1974) and Steven Spielberg's *The Sugarland Express* (1974) being key examples. They were set in America's heartland, and depicted cars spewing dust, lawmen (and civilians) wearing Stetsons, and heroes - or at least protagonists - who existed firmly outside the law. An honourable mention might be made, too, of John Trent's Canadian-made *Sunday in the Country* (aka *Vengeance is Mine* or *Blood for Blood*) (1974).

These films delighted in their landscape as much as their characters, and one of the greatest incarnations would

have to be Michael Ritchie's *Prime Cut* (1972), starring Lee Marvin and Gene Hackman.

Nick Devlin (Lee Marvin), a freelance enforcer, is sent to Kansas City by Chicago-based Irish mobsters to collect an outstanding debt owed by Mary Ann (Gene Hackman). Along the way he rescues/adopts Poppy (Sissy Spacek), an orphan who has been groomed as a sex-slave. When Poppy is taken by Mary Ann and his psychotic brother Weenie (Gregory Walcott), Devlin's mission becomes as much personal as professional.

The opening sequence of *Prime Cut* is one of its most celebrated moments, showing a human corpse being fed through a slaughterhouse and finally emerging as a string of sausages. It sets the tone for the film that follows - brutal and blackly comic.

In spite of its lush scenery and vivid colours (the vast prairie land of Alberta standing in for the wheat-fields of Kansas) and its fascination with the minutiae of Heartland Americana, *Prime Cut* is at heart a dark and often disturbing film.

Human-meat sausages notwithstanding, there are equally depraved elements involving human trafficking, sex-slavery and gang-rape. A previous enforcer, we are told, was found "in ten feet of cow flop", another "floating down the Missouri", and naked, drugged young women are exhibited like livestock in straw-strewn pens prior to auction.

By rights, Mary Ann and Weenie – 'the pigsfoot brothers' - should be comical figures (if only because of their names) but Hackman and Walcott play them with gleeful savagery, the former with a chilling bonhomie and the latter with a manic intensity which wouldn't have been out of place in Tobe Hooper's *The Texas Chainsaw Massacre* (1974).

Walcott's performance is outstanding, constantly chomping on hotdogs (hence his nickname), living high on the hog in a flophouse, threatening to turn Devlin and his men into "Irish stew, then grease!" At one point he and Hackman engage in a brotherly brawl, inflicting pain and insults on each other just for the fun of it ("You old wart", "You old cheese", "Goddam old weevil, you", "Turd head", "Old skinny shit!") like overgrown children who steadfastly refuse to mature. Best known, unfairly, as the male star of Ed Wood's notorious *Plan 9 from Outer Space* (1959), Walcott was always a solid and dependable actor, and *Prime Cut* is his finest screen performance.

Hackman, although second-billed, has relatively little screen time (this is Lee Marvin's movie, after all) but doesn't waste a second of it. We first see him feasting on a plate of steaming cow guts ("I like 'em!"), eyes twinkling, a smile never far from his lips. But when Devlin interrupts his meal, a look of pure fury passes across his face before being quickly replaced with the smiling, twinkling mask.

A series of roles in such films as *Bonnie and Clyde* and *The Split* (1968) had established his formidable screen presence, but the success of William Friedkin's multi-Oscar winning *The French Connection* (1971) brought him to widespread prominence and acclaim.

But, as has been noted, *Prime Cut* is Lee Marvin's film - his name appearing on screen before the title - and his cold, still performance dominates it. Marvin was an actor who knew how to use the camera and had honed his craft working with directors like John Sturges (*Bad Day at Black Rock*, 1955), Budd Boetticher (*Seven Men from Now*, 1956) Michael Curtiz (*The Comancheros*, 1961) and John Ford (*The Man Who Shot Liberty Valance*, 1962, *Donovan's Reef*, 1963). His Oscar-winning turn in Elliot Silverstein's *Cat Ballou* (1965), as the drunken gunfighter Kid Shelleen and his tin-nosed nemesis Tim Strawn, transformed him into an eminently bankable star. The scenes between Devlin and Mary Ann are intense, as if the actors themselves are sparring with each other as much as their characters. Hackman's Irresistible Force meets Marvin's Immovable Object, and the threat of deadly violence crackles in the air throughout.

Devlin is capable of tenderness as well, as shown when he rescues Poppy from Mary Ann's clutches (an action that has the added bonus of further riling an already annoyed Mary Ann). He becomes a father figure to her as the film progresses. Devlin may be a killer, but he is a professional and his particular brand of evil is worlds removed from that practised by the pigsfoot brothers. Marvin does a lot with small movements and gestures - a wintry smile is enough to reprimand a disapproving couple when he takes Poppy to dinner, for example - and the look on his face when he discovers the horribly abused Violet (Janit Baldwin), sold to the flophouse bums by Weenie ("He said they could love me for a nickle"), has a burning, immobile intensity which launches the film into its 'gathering storm' climax.

Prime Cut also marked the big-screen debut of Sissy Spacek who portrays Poppy as fragile and almost bewildered, a child born into a world she doesn't fully understand but which, she knows, means her harm. It is

hardly surprising she readily accepts Devlin as her knight errant.

The performances in *Prime Cut* are exemplary. The horror of her existence (and, by extension, the existence of the other girls held by Mary Ann and Weenie in a hothouse like so many orchids) is plain to see on Violet's face. Angel Tompkins, as Mary Ann's perfidious wife Clarabelle, brings her all to a relatively brief but hugely important role. Equally, William Morey as Devlin's loyal sidekick, Shay, elevates a minor role into something special.

There are moments of sheer visual poetry. Ritchie allows his camera to linger when it needs to, and the cinematography by Gene Polito is often stunning. The bright lights and eccentricities of nocturnal Chicago are contrasted with the sunny and equally eccentric Kansas City. There are times when the characters are dwarfed by the landscape, reduced to mere dots: the joy of a local fair becomes a deadly chase, then an even deadlier one in the wheat-fields when Devlin and Poppy are chased by a combine harvester.

Richie delights in his rural setting. Mary Ann's men wear bib-overalls and carry shotguns and rifles as a weapon of choice. Sequences are shot in seemingly endless sunflower fields. Equally, the title sequence - following the processes of the slaughterhouse - has a stark modernism to it, dwelling on the machines that process meat.

The combine harvester chase is another of the film's celebrated moments, and Richie takes his time with it, turning the agricultural machine into a thing of pure horror, demonstrating its destructive power when Devlin and Poppy are saved by Shay crashing a car into its jaws and letting the camera capture rending metal, crapped out the other end as a metal/straw hybrid.

A note must be made about Lalo Schifrin's extraordinary score. Schifrin was the doyen of Hollywood composers in

LEE MARVIN & GENE HACKMAN

TOGETHER THEY'RE MURDER

"PRIME CUT"

LEE MARVIN · GENE HACKMAN in "PRIME CUT" A CINEMA CENTER FILMS PRESENTATION
ALSO STARRING GREGORY WALCOTT AND ANGEL TOMPKINS · WRITTEN BY ROBERT DILLON
A JOE WIZAN PRODUCTION · EXECUTIVE PRODUCER—KENNETH L. EVANS · DIRECTED BY MICHAEL RITCHIE
MUSIC BY LALO SCHIFRIN · PANAVISION · TECHNICOLOR · A NATIONAL GENERAL PICTURES RELEASE
R RESTRICTED Under 17 requires accompanying Parent or Adult Guardian

the late '60s, well into the '70s, and brought his distinctive sound to such films as Peter Yates' *Bullitt* (1968), Don Siegel's *Coogan's Bluff* (1968), Brian G. Hutton's *Kelly's Heroes* (1970) and Siegel's *Dirty Harry* (1971). The music of *Prime Cut* - from the gentle muzak of the title sequence, to the apocalyptic final scenes where Marvin's entrance is literally punctuated with a thunderclap - is constantly in motion. There are no musical themes to speak of, no identifiable leitmotifs for hero or villain, but the score continually shifts and adapts to the film itself.

At the time of its release, *Prime Cut* was criticised for its violence, but more is implied than shown and the film's sense of dark morality probably had more to do with its negative reception than anything else. When Devlin forces open Violet's hand and a dozen or more coins spill out, it gives an horrific coda to her story and one which is much more powerful than if we had voyeuristically witnessed it on screen. Similarly, the death of one of Devlin's men and the abduction of Poppy take place off-screen, but the knowledge that it has happened is more important in narrative terms than the actual event, and the 'human sausage' opening is anything but graphic, though it does give us a queasy picture of the process from cow to hamburger.

There is no honour among thieves here, nor does there need to be - a sentiment that had been found in Jules Dassin's *Rififi,* (1955), Stanley Kubrick's *The Killing* (1956), John Boorman's *Point Blank* (1967) and would be found again in Quentin Tarantino's *Reservoir Dogs* (1992) - but Lee Marvin provides a moral centre in a film that might otherwise have been utterly bleak.

There is at least the satisfaction of seeing Weenie and Mary Ann being brought to justice (albeit Mob justice). After a lengthy and costly gunfight in a sunflower field, Devlin finds himself alone (as is only right for the star of the picture) and crashes through gates and walls in a hijacked articulated truck, just as the lightning ends and the torrents of rain begin.

Marvin had seen combat during the Second World War, being wounded at least twice, and brought an authenticity to his roles by drawing from those experiences. Like Major Reisman in *The Dirty Dozen* (1967), Devlin tapes two magazines together for his machine-gun and there is more than a sense that he has seen too much violence already.

In the final shoot-out, Devlin guns down numerous henchmen before fatally wounding both Mary Ann and Weenie. Mary Ann falls into a pig pen while Weenie, utterly enraged, nearly kills Devlin but (comically) stabs him with a hot-dog rather than a knife before succumbing to his wounds.

One of the most understated moments, possibly heavily edited, is the death of Mary Ann. Conventional criticism has it that, badly wounded and unable to take the pain, Mary Ann begs Devlin to kill him. There is another reading, however, more hinted at than displayed, and that is that Mary Ann has been castrated either by Devlin's bullets or by the pig. Certainly, Hackman's reaction in his death scene would imply one or the other (probably castration by pig, which would sit well, and provide great dramatic irony, with the rest of the film), and Devlin's refusal to deliver the *coup de grace* is the act of a man who is not content with simple vengeance.

And that's where the film should end, but there's a twee coda where Poppy's fellow orphans are rescued and she is able to punch the presumably complicit matron by way of retribution while the liberated orphans skip happily through the fields. All notion of what happened to Violet and the other girls already sold is forgotten as Marvin and Spacek head for Los Angeles, "as peaceful as any place anywhere."

Michael Ritchie made his directorial debut in 1969 with *Downhill Racer*, starring Robert Redford and Gene Hackman. A capable journeyman rather than an auteur, he made a few notable films - *The Candidate* (1972), *The Bad News Bears* (1976), *Semi-Tough* (1977), the bonkers pirate horror *The Island* (1980) and the Chevy Chase comedy *Fletch* (1985) - but by the end of his career had become a hired hand, helming such lightweight fare as *Cops & Robbersons* (1994) which saw the unlikely pairing of Jack Palance and Chevy Chase.

Prime Cut is his best film by a country mile, one of the most brutal of the '70s and, equally, one of the decade's most visually eloquent.

by Peter Sawford

Almost since the invention of motion pictures, filmmakers have looked to history or current events for inspiration and ideas. Both have proven a great source of material for filmmakers and writers alike. A good example is *Juggernaut* (1974), which was loosely inspired by a bomb scare on the luxury liner *QE2* in 1972.

Ordered by the Cunard Line, the *QE2* was 76,000 tonnes of pure opulence - the most luxurious ship afloat; the liner of choice for royalty, movie stars and other celebrities looking for a sedate, lavish and pampered way to travel across the Atlantic. In May 1972, the *QE2* was sailing from New York to Southampton when an anonymous phone call was received at the Cunard Line's New York office claiming bombs had been placed aboard. Unless a ransom of $1m was paid, they would be detonated, irreparably damaging and possibly sinking the ship. After a discreet but thorough search, no bombs were found. The British Government decided not to take any chances, and dispatched a plane carrying four bomb disposal specialists to parachute aboard and carry out a second search (which also proved negative).

Back in New York, the FBI swiftly arrested a suspect and the *QE2* continued its journey, its four extra passengers enjoying an unexpected but low-key voyage to Britain. For any writer or producer looking for a great idea for a film, this was like manna from heaven. Just two years later, *Juggernaut* hit the big screen.

The film was the brainchild of David Picker, former head of production at United Artists. A script was written by Richard Alan Simmons, who also agreed to serve as producer. One of his first tasks was to find the right director, and he opted for Richard Lester.

Born in Philadelphia, Lester had moved to England in 1955 and was picked by Peter Sellers to direct *The Running, Jumping and Standing Still Film* (1959), a comedy short devised by Sellers and Spike Milligan. That film proved such a firm favourite with all four Beatles that they hired Lester to direct *A Hard Day's Night* in 1964 and *Help!* the following year.

Throughout the '60s, Lester mainly made comedies such as *The Mouse on the Moon* (1963), *The Knack… and How to Get It* (1965) and *A Funny Thing Happened on the Way to the Forum* (1966). He arrived on the set of *Juggernaut* having just worked on the serio-comic swashbuckler *The Three Musketeers* (1973). Lester was a man who liked to work at pace, to keep on (or ahead of) schedule, and this no-nonsense approach lends *Juggernaut* an edge and a much-needed sense of urgency.

Some of the main casting had already been done by the time Lester was hired. Richard Harris and David Hemmings, two of the biggest stars of the British screen at the time, were already signed, but the biggest coup was getting Omar Sharif as Captain Brunel. A star of international standing since his brilliant entrance in David Lean's 1962 classic *Lawrence of Arabia*, Sharif's name on billboards and posters was worth its weight in gold. Although not yet global stars, both Anthony Hopkins and Ian Holm were soon attached too. Next, Lester set about hiring some of the best character actors from both sides of the Atlantic, the likes of Shirley Knight, Clifton James,

Roy Kinnear, Freddie Jones, Julian Glover and Jack Watson. But the director's main focus before starting filming was to amend the script.

Almost as soon as he was hired, Lester contacted British playwright Alan Plater to redraft and improve the screenplay. This was, remember, a screenplay that had been written by Richard Alan Simmons, the film's producer, so ordering a complete revamp of what Simmons had written was a bold move by Lester to say the least.

Plater had worked mainly in British television but was skilled at creating characters who were believable and recognisable to the viewing public. He wasn't known for writing great action-packed stories, but that didn't matter in *Juggernaut* because the dramatic aspects practically wrote themselves. One of the great bonuses of Plater's script is the way he makes us genuinely care about the various characters, identifying with them as events escalate.

There were still two pieces of the jigsaw to put in place before the cameras could start rolling - extras were needed to play the ship's passengers and crew, and, more importantly, an actual ship was required to film on. The *TS Hamburg* was a 25,000-tonne cruise ship which had taken to the seas for the first time in 1969. It had recently been sold to the Black Sea Shipping Company and renamed *Maxim Gorky*. It was chartered by Simmons for the duration of the shoot. An essential aspect of the storyline was that the vessel would be sailing in foul weather. Since the Atlantic couldn't be counted on to provide endlessly choppy conditions, it was decided to carry out filming in the North Sea which was better known for its wild weather. Newspaper advertisements were run across Britain asking for extras who were prepared and able to participate in a lengthy cruise on the North Sea during March and April 1974. The ads made it abundantly clear the ship would be actively seeking the worst weather the North Sea could throw at them - only those with strong stomachs need apply! Nevertheless, over 2,500 people came forth and these were finally whittled down to 250.

In order to keep the runtime under two hours, Lester couldn't afford to waste too much time on exposition or backstory, so he tells the story briskly and leanly on two fronts. First, we watch the events unfolding aboard the liner, including the locating and defusing of the bombs; secondly, back in Britain, we observe Scotland Yard officers as they desperately hunt for the bomber.

The anonymous caller, referring to himself as Juggernaut, informs Nicholas Porter (Ian Holm) - head of the fictitious Sovereign Line - that the Sovereign ship *SS Britannic*, which has just set sail for America, has seven bombs aboard. These will be detonated unless he's paid £500,000. Scotland Yard is tasked with tracking down Juggernaut. At the same time, the government flies a team of bomb disposal experts - headed by Lt-Commander Tony Fallon

(Richard Harris) and Charlie Braddock (David Hemmings) - to the ship to see if the bombs can be defused.

The long arm of Scotland Yard is represented by Supt. John McCleod (Anthony Hopkins), who reveals to Porter that his wife Susan (Caroline Mortimer) and two children (real-life brother and sister Adam and Rebecca Bridge), are aboard the endangered ship. This aspect of the plot is clearly designed to raise the emotional stakes and add an extra dimension to McCleod's hunt for Juggernaut, but it does neither. In fact, it actually detracts from (rather than enhancing) the tension. McCleod never seems overly upset or concerned about the fate of his wife and kids. Some of that may be down to the character's professional attitude, but one has to wonder if their relationship has lost some of its lustre and is heading for the rocks. If so, it needed explaining better. Either way, this plot element doesn't generate the intended additional suspense.

McCleod and his team, including second-in-command Detective Brown (played by the wonderful Kenneth Colley), start to work their way through the bomb and explosives experts on an Armed Forces and government watchlist. Hopkins and Colley make an amusing double act, swapping acidic comments and sarcastic remarks as they hunt for the deadly bomber. Moreover, their chase leads to two wonderful cameos. First is Major O'Neil, an implied IRA member played by Cyril Cusack, who delights in dangling McCleod on a piece of string before quietly declaring that he doesn't care what happens to the ship. He has no hope of parole and expresses no interest in helping the very government that's imprisoned him. His conscience will remain clear; he won't lose any sleep whether the *Britannic* survives or sinks. Cusack's tone and demeanour never change during his short scene; he conveys absolute hatred for the British and total disregard for the lives of the passengers on the imperilled ship. Next, Brown meets Mr. Baker (Michael Hordern), a mercenary specialising in explosives. Baker proudly declares he only ever works abroad (as if that makes his destructive line of work okay) and points out that his "last job was actually for the British government." Hordern subtly blurs the lines between good-terrorist, bad-terrorist and anti-terrorist in just a few short sentences.

From the moment the *Britannic* sets sail, the weather in the North Atlantic is appalling. Filming in the North Sea may have caused all sorts of individual challenges, but it was well worth it. The shots of the ship pitching and rolling in the rough swell are enough to make viewers with the very best sea legs long for solid ground. I can only imagine what the cast and crew must have felt suffering in such conditions 24 hours a day.

Once aboard, Fallon and Braddock are tasked with locating and defusing Juggernaut's bombs. The relationship between them is established in just a few moments. Fallon and Braddock's friendship has been forged in the

most extreme adversity and is based on mutual respect and admiration. Unsurprisingly, their sense of humour is pitch-black, the grimmest gallows humour imaginable. They trust each other implicitly and know that one slip, one mistake, one error of judgement will mean goodbye world, hello oblivion.

Throughout the film, we get a good look into the psyche of the men who work in bomb disposal and the minds of those who build the very devices the disposal boys strive to defuse. Although acutely aware of the danger, Fallon and Braddock like to live on the edge and only feel fully alive when they're potentially seconds from death. Both are aware they'll most likely retire in a loud bang and a ball of flame, yet still they're addicted to the dangerous job they do.

When Fallon meets Captain Brunel, they discuss Juggernaut's motives and Brunel points out that the line between those who *make* and those who *defuse* bombs is indistinguishable. He considers them both as obsessed as each other. Fallon's safety valve is his humour. He meets every problem, every danger, with a wry comment or a sarcastic joke. When one of bombs explodes, taking Braddock with it, even Fallon finds his humorous façade failing. In an outburst to Captain Brunel, he admits (possibly for the first time in his life) that his courage has a limit, that his seemingly iron nerve has a breaking point. The idea of failing, so long anathema to him, suddenly seems the only sensible route. "The saboteur has won," he seems to infer, though he stops short of saying it. "Just pay the man, and let's all move on with our lives." After

drinking half a bottle of Scotch, then smashing it against the cabin wall, Fallon re-adjusts his sights and gets back to the task. Deep down, we know he hates to lose; plus, of course, his thirst to avenge Braddock keeps his hands steady.

The scenes depicting the men working to deactivate the bombs are superbly filmed. As each screw is slowly turned allowing access to the inner workings of the bomb, we in the audience, like the men next to the barrels, feel our palms getting sweatier by the second. Lester positions his camera right inside the barrels to show the intricacies of the devices and the problems Juggernaut has set for Fallon and his team. A maze of wires, connections, running metal tape and dead ends all require negotiating before Fallon can proudly chant his favourite motto: "Fallon's the champion!"

Richard Harris is perfectly cast as Fallon. His Irish roots bring a sardonic, slightly fatalistic element to the role. He never seemed the sort of actor who took life completely seriously and he brings this element of his own persona to the role. In a substantially smaller role, David Hemmings makes the best of what he has. His ready wit and equally laidback view of life and work makes Charlie Braddock a very likeable character. Because of this, his demise packs a wallop and feels like a genuinely sad loss. Anthony Hopkins is well cast as the diligent, slightly world-weary policeman determined to stop Juggernaut, but doubtful it can be achieved in the short timeframe. Ian Holm looks totally at home as the harassed head of the cruise line who wants to end everything as quickly as possible.

The first time I saw the film, I thought Omar Sharif played a somewhat peripheral character. But on more recent viewings, it's clear to me his performance is much more nuanced than I noticed initially. He portrays a man who's used to being in complete command on his vessel yet finds himself suddenly side-lined by events and must accept that control of the ship now belongs to Juggernaut (and hopefully, ultimately, to Fallon). The role of Juggernaut/Sid Buckland is a small one and early on mainly consists of a voice on the phone. The fact that he's such a memorable villain is testament to the talent of Freddie Jones. Jones makes Buckland scarily calm and controlled throughout. He's faced death a hundred times in the service of his country only to be thrown on the scrapheap with a pittance of a pension and the mental scars that were considered part and parcel of the job. Playing Buckland is almost a trial run for Jones' magnificently malevolent performance as Bytes in David Lynch's The Elephant Man (1980). Shirley Knight, a wonderful character actress who never gets the credit she deserves, is slightly wasted as a passenger named Mrs Bannister. Her relationship with the Captain never goes anywhere and her character doesn't influence anything. Devoting time to her is as big a misstep as McCleod's wife being on board the stricken ship. Fallon's

boss is played with disciplined simplicity by Julian Glover, while the officious, bureaucratic, slightly condescending government representative is the sort of character John Stride could play in his sleep.

Despite all these fine performances, there are two I believe deserve individual praise. Born in Spokane, Washington in 1920 and a decorated World War 2 veteran, Clifton James was probably best known in Britain for his two performances as sheriff J.W. Pepper in Roger Moore's first Bond outing Live and Let Die (1973) and the slightly cringeworthy reprise in The Man with the Golden Gun (1974). In point of fact, James had been a hardworking, well-respected actor for many years in films like Cool Hand Luke (1967), Will Penny (1967) and The New Centurions (1972). As Corrigan, the Mayor of a substantial town in America, James could easily have fallen back into Sheriff Pepper territory. Instead, he turns in a performance of great richness and restraint, with plenty of memorable moments. He's one of the first to fully realise something is seriously wrong aboard the ship, but instead of demanding answers he simply asks questions, quietly accepting that everything that can be done is being done. He's happy to do what's asked of him. Being a seasoned politician, he admits he knows only too well how to lie and how to spot a lie when it bites him. Twice he comments to 3rd Officer Hardy (Andy Bradford): "I believe I've just been bitten." At the fancy dress party, his wife (Doris Nolan) asks him if he's ever been unfaithful. Corrigan answers that he hasn't since they've been married, but that he was once after they met. Without another word, James shows his relief at finally unloading himself of the guilt he's carried around with him for years. But it's clear he hates himself for what he did, and he carries a certain anger at the fact that a previous moment of stupidity hurts his beloved wife. It's a short but beautifully judged performance from an actor who would go on to grace films such as The Untouchables (1987), Eight Men Out (1988) and The Bonfire of the Vanities (1990) before his death in 1996.

Roy Kinnear was a much-loved and versatile star of television and film in Britain. Making his breakthrough in That Was the Week That Was in 1962, Kinnear appeared in several British sit-coms as well as the variety style shows of Dick Emery and Stanley Baxter. He had previously worked extensively with Richard Lester and had literally followed him to the set of Juggernaut from The Three Musketeers. As Social Director Curtain, Kinnear is responsible for some of the film's best laugh-out-loud moments as well as one of its most poignant. Early on during the cruise, Curtain knows he's up against it if he is to keep the passengers amused. His jokes fall flat, his jolliness is largely ignored, and only the other members of the crew seem to appreciate his efforts. Curtain continues to try and keep spirits up until halfway through the fancy dress evening he finally gives up and with a resigned "Sod 'em" heads to the bar for two large whiskies in the same glass. It's here that he chats to Mrs Bannister, and Kinnear and Knight are given the chance to share a marvellous scene. Mrs Bannister, tired that her affair with the Captain is going nowhere, sympathises with Curtain's situation and tells him he's doing a wonderful job, but Curtain isn't in the mood to be patronised and admits to being frightened. The clowns mask he's been wearing finally slips to reveal a man as worried and scared as everyone else aboard, but unable to show it until that moment. Kinnear plays it perfectly, never coming across as petulant or angry, just tired of pretending that everything is under control, exhausted by the burden of endless cheerfulness. Mrs Bannister willingly agrees to his request for a dance and, in a touching scene, the pair make their way around the dance floor. Unexpectedly, everyone suddenly starts to join them having been finally stirred out of their apathy. At his lowest moment, Curtain has his moment of triumph, inadvertently achieving his goal of bringing everyone together and creating a party atmosphere in the unlikeliest circumstances imaginable.

Principal filming took place between March and April 1974. Although scheduled for ten weeks, Lester's no-nonsense style meant everything was done within six. There are some lovely moments of humour in the film. At lunch on the first full day at sea, plates of food are served up in the kitchens, carried out to the restaurant and just as quickly sent back by seasick passengers who quickly seek the sanctuary of their cabins and their en-suite toilets; McCleod's children play on a slot machine called *Shipwreck*; the 3rd Officer, Hardy, goes to light a cigarette and then rethinks the sanity of sparking a lighter next to 7000lbs of high explosives.

Despite these snatches of humour, not everyone was laughing behind the scenes. The producer and original screenwriter Richard Alan Simmons was so angered by the script alterations that he had his name taken off the film and only later accepted a credit under the name of Richard DeKocker.

Cinematographer Gerry Fisher - who would go on to work on such fine films as *Aces High* (1976) and *Highlander* (1986) - doesn't disappoint. His camerawork is excellent throughout, from the busy hub of activity in London to the close-up views of the bombs, the intricate wiring and the beads of sweat on nervous foreheads. His camera never seems to intrude, remaining at a detached distance except when he takes it inside the barrels and gives us a window into Fallon's world of complex mechanisms and tripwires.

Most of the music in the film is organic. As the ship prepares to set sail at the beginning, it is sent on its way by a brass band and a Highland Pipes band. During the voyage, the only music we hear is piped through the ship's loudspeaker system or played by the ship's band (during the fancy dress party, for example). In fact, throughout the entire film there are only four moments of scored music credited to Ken Thorne. On the first three occasions, Thorne's music works well, heightening tension and adding to the anxiety and stress of the scenes. It's a shame his scoring wasn't used a little more during the film. The final piece of music plays out over the end credits as Fallon quietly smokes his pipe and reflects on another successful job, but also the loss of his close friend and colleague. It's a gentle, almost melancholic theme, hinting at the relief the passengers and crew are feeling but also the incalculable loss Fallon has suffered.

Released in the US on 25th September 1974, and on 10th October in the UK, *Juggernaut* flopped on its initial run. Although it wasn't savaged by the critics, it wasn't exactly praised to the skies either. Lester always believed this was because it was misleadingly promoted as an action film. *Juggernaut* has tension by the bucketload, but action? Six men sitting next to barrels, slowly taking screws out of a plate, cannot be described as action. I'm sure many people left the cinema when it was all over feeling cheated. Even the arrest of Juggernaut occurs very quietly and with a minimum of fuss.

I think, though, that there were other factors at play too. In 1974, we were living in a world where terrorism was on the front page of newspapers almost every day. Terrorist threats or acts were continually being reported on television and was almost certainly in the backs of anyone's mind. Perhaps cinema audiences had had their fill of bombs, threats and terror. It's a huge shame the film didn't find a better audience as it's well-directed, well-acted and edgy, with believable characters and a plot that constantly keeps you on your toes and the edge of your nerves.

Juggernaut has been released on both DVD and Blu-ray, sometimes under its optional title *Terror on the Britannic*. Thusfar, we are yet to have a definitive director's cut released. Hopefully, somewhere, there's an executive who feels *Juggernaut* has been poorly served by its previous releases. Before it's too late, that elusive exec might organise a re-issue with commentaries from Lester and some of the surviving cast. The film fully deserves such treatment and has done for some time. It's a great suspense piece and it absolutely screams out for a bells-and-whistle Blu-ray release.

Caricatures by Aaron Stielstra

Florinda Bolkan in *Investigation of a Citizen Above Suspicion* (pg. 44)

Ralph Meeker in *Food of the Gods* (pg. 82)

Tomas Milian in *Four of the Apocalypse* (pg. 34)

John Wayne in *The Shootiist* (pg. 79)

Honor Blackman in *The Cat and the Canary* (pg. 92)

Gian Maria Volonte in *Investigation of a Citizen Above Suspicion* (pg. 44)

Roman Polanski's
film of
MACBETH

by Steven West

Fair is foul and foul is fair.

There was more than one provocative version of *Macbeth* doing the rounds in Britain in 1972. Peter Coe's stage production of *Black Macbeth* was set in tribal Africa rather than 12th century Scotland and had an all-black cast. The lead, played by Oscar James, was renamed Mbeth, and juju men were used in place of the witches. It was inspired by Coe's theory that the story could be shifted to any time or place where tribal life and the belief in witchcraft endured. It was the latest experimental take on the Bard to be put on at London's Roundhouse theatre, preceded by a musical version of *Othello* which incorporated Louisiana swamp rock. Speaking on Humphrey Burton's arts show *Aquarius*, Coe was slightly sarcastic about his fellow guest Roman Polanski, whose own adaptation - a big-screen rendition - was also on national release in the UK that February. He referred to Polanski's version as "Oh! Caledonia!" and, in a mocking nod to the director's youthful leads, called it a "Scottish star-crossed lovers piece."

'Variety' positioned the film as the 16th known screen version of *Macbeth* (most sources pinpoint the first as emerging in 1908). With the world's attention focused on its director for tragic real-life reasons, scepticism was rife. The first onscreen text reinforced this scepticism: "Columbia Pictures Presents: A Playboy Production of Roman Polanski's Film...The Tragedy of Macbeth."

For me, Polanski's *Macbeth* evokes adolescent classroom memories not dissimilar to those I have of the raunchy interactions between buff Leonard Whiting and buxom Olivia Hussey in Franco Zeffirelli's 1968 version of *Romeo and Juliet*. Polanski's take on the accursed 'Scottish Play' seemed to me and my classmates (a set of particularly spotty and horny early '90s teenagers) a most welcome 15-rated attempt to "make Shakespeare hot again". Moreover, we probably didn't appreciate at the time that we were witnessing the first and only time names like William Shakespeare, Roman Polanski, Hugh Hefner and Keith Chegwin would appear in the same opening credits sequence!

Orchestrated by a bungling teacher who was seemingly using a VCR for the first time, my schoolmates and I had a pre-existing penchant for gruesome fare and thus found the screening of the film very appealing. After an early sight of the rising sun turning the sky appropriately blood-red, we were treated to a couple of hours of murdered kids, massacres, ghosts, hangings, and hubbling and bubbling from some suitably grotesque witches. It was as close as we'd ever get to being allowed to watch *Witchfinder General* in secondary school, deliciously rife with severed arms, spooky castle interiors, torrential rain, Gothic fog, plus a youthful Lady Macbeth appearing nude! It also featured the first great decapitation of '70s cinema, a decade in which big-screen beheadings would outshine previous bonce-bouncers in the likes of *Dementia 13* (1963) and *Strait-Jacket* (1964).

Like the fruitier late-night Hammer movies on TV and that racy Sabrina music video (if you know, you know), this screening of *Macbeth* at school was a 'Dear Diary' moment for sure.

All of Them Witches.

Inevitably, early '70s critics were notably colder in their reception than a bunch of teens enjoying cinematic flesh and gore in the lesson after double maths. Nonplussed by

early cuts, Columbia pushed for significant alterations and preview screenings. They ultimately abandoned a planned December 1971 Royal Command Performance and opted to premiere *Macbeth* at Hefner's new New York Playboy Theatre. A "suicidal" (Polanski's word) wide release followed in the commercial graveyard period that was January, and to no-one's great surprise it didn't trouble *Diamonds are Forever* in the slightest at the box office.

Roger Ebert and Judith Crist found much to admire, but some US reviewers seemed childishly fixated on the 'Playboy' involvement, making cheap jibes about upmarket source material being overseen by downmarket producers. "[Francesca] Annis comes across like a spot-crazy 'Playboy' bunny," carped the 'New York Daily Mirror', while at least one critic joshed about looking for staples in the middle of the screen. The personal losses suffered by its director were tastelessly invoked. The Tate/La-Bianca murder trial had commenced in the summer of 1970 (when *Macbeth* was in pre-production), and one relatively positive writer couldn't resist making a link, calling it: "A work of art - in the grand manner of Buchenwald, Lidice and, yes, the Manson murders." Others considered the violence to be in poor taste following one of Hollywood's darkest hours, even though such gruesomeness was inherent in the centuries-old play. 'Time' magazine, who had made Polanski their 'Face of European Cinema' on the cover of a 1963 issue, bemoaned the emphasis on the supernatural (perhaps forgetting its prominent place in the original text): "So unrestrained that many of the straight scenes have an almost cursory air," they remarked.

All this sound and fury signified nothing, and the film's reputation has continued to grow over the decades. In some ways, Polanski had been due a backlash because, as we all know, success usually breeds contempt, and his *Knife in the Water* (1962) had been Oscar nominated while his English-language debut *Repulsion* (1965) and freshman Hollywood effort *Rosemary's Baby* (1968) had won many admirers. The 1969 tragedy at Cielo Drive merely hastened the attacks from notepad warriors who, in any case, were bound to turn against him at some point. Polanski knew that returning to directing after the infamous murders was a no-win situation. "Whatever film I'd come out with next would have been treated the same way," he observed, adding that a knockabout comedy (which he made next,

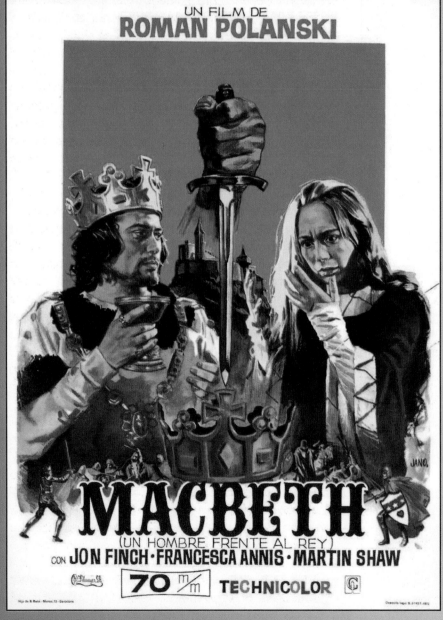

UN FILM DE
ROMAN POLANSKI

MACBETH
(UN HOMBRE FRENTE AL REY)
CON JON FINCH · FRANCESCA ANNIS · MARTIN SHAW
70 m/m TECHNICOLOR

with *What?*) would have been accused of insensitivity. Shakespeare was deemed a safe option to preserve his motives from suspicion, but many assumed he chose this particular play because it was incredibly dark and offered a form of cinematic catharsis.

Horror and violence had always been present in both Polanski's life and films. Early shorts like *Murder* and *Teeth Smile* focused on home invasion, voyeurism and random brutality. His earliest feature films were mostly containment thrillers with downbeat endings, such as the two he did for Tony Tenser and Michael Klinger at Compton (*Repulsion* and *Cul-de-sac*). Despite their genre trappings, they were far from the commercial horrors everyone anticipated. Critical adoration would return with *Chinatown* (1974), ironically hailed for its stunningly pessimistic conclusion and a moment of cringe-inducing violence which everyone remembers.

Something Wicked This Way Comes.

With Tuesday Weld declining (reportedly due to the nudity) and Marianne Faithful testing but struggling with the lines, Francesca Annis - who had appeared in Compton's *The Pleasure Girls* (1965) and was Klinger's first choice for the unhinged heroine in *Repulsion* - joined as Lady Macbeth after shooting began. Polanski had seen her in *The Heretic* in the West End, and knew she would satisfy his desire to avoid making a filmed play "for geriatrics, with Macbeth as an old gangster and Lady Macbeth as an old hag." Jon Finch, fresh from the Hammer entries *The Vampire Lovers* and *The Horror of Frankenstein* (1970) and en route to Hitchcock's *Frenzy* (1972), was in his late twenties when he first encountered Polanski on a plane. The younger Annis would subvert convention by playing Lady Macbeth *before* essaying Juliet (opposite Ian McKellen at the RSC in 1976), though skewing younger was not without precedent: Orson Welles was just 33 when playing the role in 1948 and Janet Suzman had just turned 30 when cast as 'Lady' in BBC's *Play of the Month*, screened in September 1970.

Elsewhere, three unfamiliar actresses from around the UK were cast as the weird sisters, while Stephen Chase (who'd played Vincent Price's rapist/witch-hunter son in the 1970 flick *Cry of the Banshee*), proved an authentic King Duncan. Rising TV and stage actor Martin Shaw was a charismatic choice as the doomed Banquo, and a pre-*Multi-Coloured Swap Shop* Keith Chegwin (afforded a memorable Chaucer-enhanced musical interlude) was cast as Fleance after appearing in assorted theatrical and Children's Film Foundation offerings.

Rosemary's Baby's had been set in 1965 and *The Fearless Vampire Killers* (1967) had a 19th century backdrop, so this was Polanski's third period piece. All three confirm his predilection for open endings in which evil evades defeat and prospers. He'd rejected opportunistic

occult-themed movie offers after *Rosemary's Baby*, but nevertheless his association with macabre material fed into the sensationalistic media reporting of the terrible events of August 8th, 1969. Unsubstantiated links between the victims and black magic orgies made profitable copy. The likes of 'Time' callously defined the crime scene as being "as grisly as anything depicted in Polanski's film explorations of the dark and melancholy corners of the human characters." The director, who would later describe his wife's star-studded funeral as being "like some ghastly movie premiere" (and who also mourned the sudden death of collaborator and friend, the innovative musician Krzysztof Komeda), had to keep working, fully aware anything he made from here onwards would be scrutinised for parallels to the massacre.

What bloody man is this?

The liberal use of wide-open spaces and dramatic weather conditions seemingly position *Macbeth* as the antithesis to the apartment-bound *Repulsion* and *Rosemary's Baby*, but it often feels just as claustrophobic as both. It's also as claustrophobic as Polanski's subsequent character-driven interior dramas like *The Tenant* (1976) and *Death and the Maiden* (1994). Gil Taylor, who had shot *Repulsion* and *Cul-de-sac*, tracks Finch's doomed Scottish king around his imposing Inverness castle quarters, prowling the shadowy corridors and tipping into full-blown haunted castle Gothic horror even when the ghosts are off screen. Taylor's eclectic '70s work would later include *Frenzy* (1972), *The Omen* (1976), *Star Wars* (1977) and John Badham's *Dracula* (1979).

Streamlining the original text to omit certain lines so that Lady Macbeth came across less like a "nagging bitch", Polanski's mission was to avoid staginess while making the language accessible for '70s audiences. He considered Welles' expressionistic, studio-compromised adaptation and Kurosawa's *Throne of Blood* (1957) unsuccessful cinematic interpretations, but he had the highest admiration for Olivier's screen *Hamlet* and stage *Macbeth*. He decided to borrow from his illustrious predecessor by repositioning the soliloquies in his film as interior monologues (sometimes spread over multiple scenes).

Polanski's partner-in-crime whilst adapting the play was another controversial figure, the renowned critic and National Theatre Company literary manager Kenneth Tynan. While the House of Commons stewed over his utterance of the word "fuck" on Ned Sherrin's late-night TV show *BBC-3* in 1965 and Mary Whitehouse suggested the S&M-favouring Tynan should have his arse spanked, his crusades against censorship and eagerness to shock led to a triumphant West End/Broadway run of the knowingly risqué musical *Oh! Calcutta!* which ruffled a few feathers. With *Macbeth* securing its main funding from the flourishing Playboy Empire, Tynan - an authority on Shakespeare -

shared the desire to use younger protagonists staking their futures on a prophecy. He also felt it would be wise to shift events to the real period (the 11th century) rather than Shakespeare's time. Cinema audiences would see an attractive couple who are unaware of their tragic destiny discovering that we all have human frailties while seeking the riches and happiness promised by the witches.

In thunder, lightning, or in rain?

Frank Simon's *Polanski Meets Macbeth* (1972), a behind-the-scenes documentary, offers great insights into the production, employing Portmeirion (backdrop to the innovative TV series *The Prisoner*) as a basecamp and Shepperton's huge soundstage for an elaborate castle construction. The documentary captures Hefner apparently relishing the controversy Polanski brought to the first 'Playboy'-backed feature film, though when an extra gleefully highlights that an actor maced in the early beach scene resembles Charles Manson, he is swiftly debunked by the director himself. While Polanski is shown devising his own blood formula, his regular make-up man Tom Smith, fresh from period horrors like *The Vampire Lovers*, applies detailed wounds for Banquo's post-mortem visits. The Welsh locations add production value and bring oppressive ambience to the picture but are also shown to be the source of major schedule revisions due to inclement weather, panicking horses and restricted access to the coven location. Polanski decried the failures of the "special *defects*" team in his autobiography, while *The Italian Job*'s Peter Collinson was observed hanging around the Shepperton canteen, groomed as a potential directorial replacement if time and money ran out. 'Playboy', cast and crew ultimately stayed loyal, with Hefner filling the financial gap when everything overran.

O horror, horror, horror!

Given the obvious horrors - production and otherwise - *Macbeth* remains a remarkable achievement: a vividly captured, spiralling nightmare with rare period detail (note the bear-baiting) and key elements that position it as a post-Romero/Reeve modern horror film: jarring glimpses of war wounds, executions, disquieting observations of gruesome medieval crime scenes. Despite the contemporary reviews, graphic gore is sparingly (but effectively) used. Macbeth, like Carol in *Repulsion* and Rosemary in *Rosemary's Baby*, fractures via hallucinatory visions and nightmares. These sequences are visceral successors to the famously censored impregnation interlude in *Rosemary's Baby* and Shaw's grinning, persistent, declining Banquo comes across like a precursor to John Landis' wisecracking, rotting corpse in *An American Werewolf in London*.

Duncan's murder, slightly trimmed for the 1971 AA rating, achieves much of its impact from the quiet intensity of its preamble (Polanski rarely over-used dramatic music) and the grim detail of the King waking just as Macbeth appears to pause his murderous plan. The violence is ugly and gruelling, reflecting wider genre trends - *Deliverance* and *The Last House on the Left*, for example, would emerge months after *Macbeth*'s premiere. In the same year as the gruelling home invasions of *A Clockwork Orange* and *Straw Dogs*, Polanski's rendering of the assault on the Macduff household would provide critics with an easy link to events at Cielo Drive, though its most distressing visuals exist in our imagination. It's far from melodramatic, with the disarming, vulnerable detail of the ill-fated child being freshly bathed preceding an atrocity we experience via off-camera screams, a fleetingly seen sexual assault and the hopelessness of Lady Macduff's efforts to flee. The use of music (or lack thereof) is a significant part of the film's overall impact. Experimental folk outfit Third Ear Band provide a sombre oboe melody for Lady Macbeth amongst other carefully positioned abstract cues (its founding member Glenn Sweeney, along with violinist Richard Goff and harpist Simon House, can be glimpsed at the banquet).

Finch and Annis bring conviction, intensity and a sense of pathos which seemed overlooked at the time. The naked sleepwalking scene, far from titillating (13-year-old self, be ashamed!), is a wrenching, pitiful insight into Lady Macbeth's vulnerability, a painful confirmation of her downward spiral. Endlessly washing her hands in desperate efforts to cleanse the guilt (a visual echo of that most modern and tragic movie murderer, Norman Bates), her portrayal is deftly balanced by Finch's powerful physical and mental decline from the brave, handsome general we first met.

While the naked coven scene that once prompted classroom sniggers now just makes us imagine a naked Ruth Gordon and Sidney Blackmer in some freshly uncovered alternate footage from *Rosemary's Baby*, the bloody show-stopping climax still delivers the required sucker punch. There's a remarkable, startling moment in which the camera briefly takes the viewpoint of Macbeth's freshly severed head as it is transported away by laughing, jeering bystanders. Polanski's signoff is as bleak as his earlier movies: a circular ending reinforcing that mankind is fickle and his chief weaknesses will inevitably repeat themselves, a cycle of violence without end - a very '70s horror movie ending, in other words!

It's also refreshingly unpretentious. The bid to make an accessible, modern *Macbeth* succeeds. On the aforementioned *Aquarius* episode, Peter Coe was asked to verbalise the essence of the original play, and articulately explained that he considered it a study of the criminal mind. When put on the spot and asked the same question, Polanski shrugged and admitted: "I haven't got a clue."

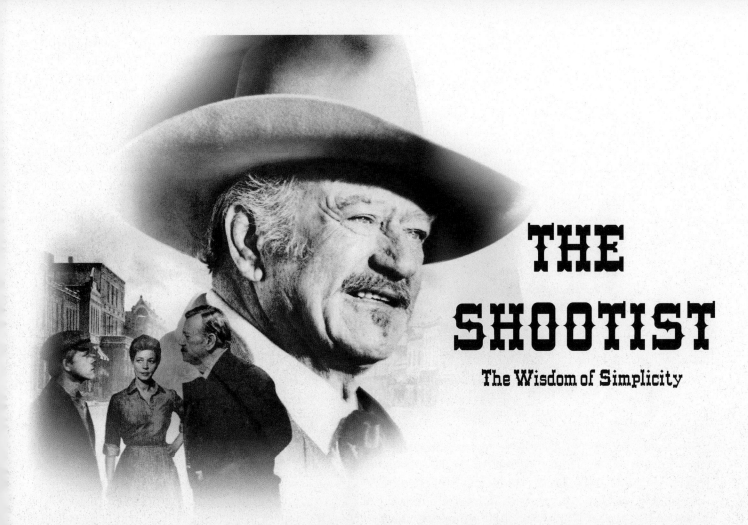

THE SHOOTIST
The Wisdom of Simplicity

Dr Andrew C. Webber reflects on ageing, regrets and the Duke's screen farewell in Don Siegel's *The Shootist* (1976).

It is to my eternal shame that in September 1976, I chose to see Alan Parker's *Bugsy Malone* at the Odeon in Rochester as opposed to Don Siegel's western *The Shootist*, starring a 70-year-old John Wayne (in what was to be his final role). To be fair, I was only 12-years-old and in the same year *had* been to the cinema to see *Shout at the Devil, A Star is Born, Burnt Offerings* (my first AA certificate), *The Eagle Has Landed* and, er, *At the Earth's Core* (which at least featured future Bond girl Caroline Munro, she of the ample cleavage whose attributes were displayed prominently on the ubiquitous Lamb's Navy Rum billboard posters of the day). I also distinctly remember having a torn ad clipping of Tinto Brass' *Salon Kitty* somewhere in my bedroom, so it wasn't all bad. But to choose *Bugsy* over the Duke is something I will always look back on with a sense of regret.

In all honesty, in 1976 the Duke was yesterday's man. If we wanted someone who was a dab hand at playing tough cowboys or dirty cops, then we had Clint Eastwood (both *The Outlaw Josey Wales* and *The Enforcer* were released that same year). Surely there was no room for some old guy in a toupee who had recently turned up in the laughable *Brannigan* (1975) and practically ruined his *True Grit* reputation (a film I *did* see on the big screen) by

making a dodgy sequel called *Rooster Cogburn* (1975), co-starring another old biddy few of us cared about at the time, Katharine Hepburn.

It would be fair to say that whilst it has its admirers, *Bugsy Malone* hasn't exactly matured with time, unlike *The Shootist* which is now considered (along with Eastwood's *The Outlaw Josey Wales*) one of the greatest films of the mid '70s and, arguably, one of the best westerns ever made.

It is based on an absolutely fantastic 1975 book by Glendon Swarthout, who also penned 'Bless the Beasts and Children' (turned into a cult film by Stanley Kramer in 1971). 'The Shootist' was adapted for the screen by Swarthout's son, Miles. It features turns by a number of Hollywood greats - Lauren Bacall, James Stewart and John Carradine all have smallish parts (as does *The Shining's* Scatman Crothers), and director Don Siegel was on a roll after *Dirty Harry* (1971), the superb *Charley Varrick* (1973) and the Michael Caine vehicle *The Black Windmill* (1974).

The novel begins brilliantly: "It was noon of a bodeful day. The sun was an eye bloodshot by dust. His horse was fistulowed." The scene is masterfully set, and the reader is immediately drawn into the world of one of the last great gunfighters (J. B. Books) who is about to learn he has only months to live.

According to Miles Swarthout, the production was troubled not only by Wayne's age and illnesses (he had, like the film's main protagonist John Bernard Books, been diagnosed with terminal cancer) but also by the fact that he and Siegel didn't really hit it off. The production was shut down for a few weeks when Wayne fell ill with flu, and when it was finally over, Swarthout Jr. tells us: "few of the principals were still speaking to one another."

Behind the scenes, several '70s stalwarts make significant contributions: Eastwood's regular cinematographer, the prolific Bruce Surtees, was behind the camera (he'd shot *The Beguiled, Play Misty for Me, Dirty Harry, Joe Kidd, High Plains Drifter* and *Josey Wales*, and also did brilliant work that decade for Bob Fosse on *Lenny* in 1974 and Arthur Penn on *Night Moves* in 1975, amongst others). Elmer Bernstein wrote the score. The editing was done by Douglas Stewart, who would win an Academy Award for his work on *The Right Stuff* in 1983, having collaborated with *Stuff's* director Phil Kaufman on all three of his '70s films - *The Great Northfield Minnesota Raid* (1972), *The White Dawn* (1974) and *Invasion of the Body Snatchers* (1978).

Sheree North, a criminally undervalued character actor who had become a bit of a regular for Siegel (she can also be seen in *Madigan, Charley Varrick* and *Telefon*), turns up as Books' former lover Serepta (now, like practically everyone else in what's left of Books' life, a money-grabbin' sumbitch). There's also Ron Howard (who'd previously played a very similar role in 1974 alongside Lee Marvin in *The Spikes Gang*) in the important role of Gillom, a young boy enamoured with the dying gunfighter. In fact, in 2014 Swarthout Jr. even penned a sequel ('The Last Shootist') which was based on Gillom's adventures following the death of Books - and that's no spoiler. *The Shootist* is - like George Roy Hill's *Butch Cassidy and the Sundance Kid*, Sam Peckinpah's *The Wild Bunch* and *Pat Garrett and Billy the Kid*, and Walter Hill's *The Long Riders* - an elegiac western. And as is so often the case with elegiac westerns, key protagonists die. That's what gives these films their gravitas and makes them feel so much more meaningful the older you get. After all, who wouldn't want to go out in a hail of bullets in slo-mo like Peckinpah's anti-heroes, or in perfect freeze-frame like Newman and Redford?

Swarthout Jr. points out that at the time, many cinemagoers (including my younger self) balked at what he calls "granddad playing cowboy", so the film got dumped in a weak autumn box-office spot (when the American football season was well underway). He even mentions overhearing a head of marketing asking: "Where are we going to open this picture? Hospitals?" The fact that *The Shootist* went on to receive rave reviews came as something of a surprise. In fact, there was then a lot of talk at the time of the film cleaning up at the Oscars, although

it only eventually got one nomination - for Robert Boyle's Art Direction. The Academy decided the best picture of 1976 was *Rocky*, a somewhat surprising choice in a year dominated by the likes of Lumet's *Network*, Scorsese's *Taxi Driver* and Pakula's *All the President's Men*.

There's lots to love about *The Shootist* as it approaches its 50th birthday. Wayne is as brilliant as you'd hope (arguably *this* is his best performance). As in the book, the final gun battle is tense and expertly staged. The opening montage, featuring clips from Wayne's earlier movies, superbly sets the tone for what is to follow and, whilst it is definitely a film about mortality and coming to terms with the finite nature of life, it's also surprisingly funny (especially during the scenes featuring John Carradine, who had starred alongside Wayne in both *Stagecoach* in 1939 and *The Man Who Shot Liberty Valance* in 1962).

The overall effect of *The Shootist* is undeniably touching, notably when Books tells Gillom his credo for life: "I won't be wronged," he says. "I won't be insulted; I won't be laid a hand on. I don't do these things to other people, and I require the same from them." These are words to live by and you know that, in spite of his dodgy politics, these are probably things Wayne himself believed. They make a pretty good epitaph for any man (or woman) and, as you get older, you begin to fully appreciate the wisdom of their simplicity.

Finally, no account of *The Shootist* would be complete without at least one reference to the genius of Roger Coleman's illustrated British quad film poster (which now fetches large amounts on collectors' sites). It is, quite simply, magnificent - and, like the film itself, a fitting tribute to the legacy and legend of the Duke. Coleman apparently took six days to complete the design (which Sim Branaghan, in his fascinating 2006 BFI publication 'British Film Posters', described as "one of the most powerful and iconic quads of the decade"). He manages to instil his portrait of Wayne with nobility, melancholy and integrity - three characteristics dear to the heart of the film's protagonist - making it very hard to believe that the role of J. B. Books had originally been intended for George C. Scott, the actor who, in 1961, had so convincingly played 'Fast' Eddie Felson's reptilian, amoral manager in Robert Rossen's poolhall classic *The Hustler*.

WHEN ANIMALS ATTACK

THE BEST(IAL) DECADE OF NATURE STRIKES BACK MOVIES

by Ian Taylor

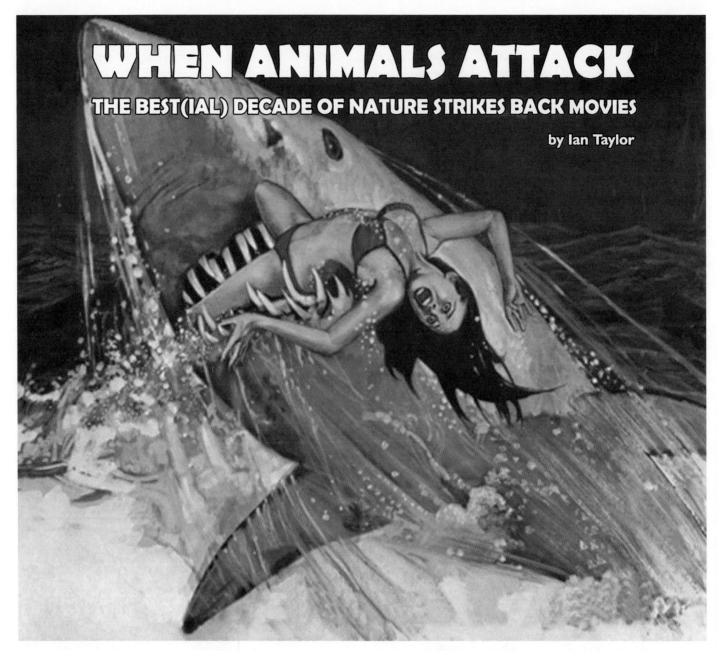

Of all the sub-genres of horror and sci-fi, it's nature running amok which always bounds back and pounces upon audiences anew.

It was surely the '70s which offered the widest variety of angry animals on the big (and small) screen, undoubtedly thanks to the deserved runaway success of *Jaws*. Of course, this is a movie that needs no introduction, but who can resist lauding an almost perfect piece of art?

Released in 1975, it catapulted director Steven Spielberg to the top. Featuring Roy Scheider as police chief Martin Brody, Robert Shaw as professional shark hunter Quint and Richard Dreyfuss as marine biologist Hooper - three disparate characters who join forces to hunt a man-eating Great White shark - it tapped into that huge fear of what might be lurking beneath the surface of the sea. The shark is attacking beachgoers at the summer resort of Amity Island but only Brody suspects the worst. Local mayor Murray Hamilton refuses to shut down the lucrative

beach and the inevitable flesh-chomping and bone-severing mayhem ensues. Despite a malfunctioning shark model, Spielberg makes it all work by focusing on character and setting, atmosphere and tension as much as overt violence or gore. The scenes shot on location at Martha's Vineyard in Massachusetts create a persuasive sense of community, and the ocean-bound sequences (the first for a major movie) are worth the budgetary and scheduling issues. The director opted to suggest the shark's presence, and composer John Williams was entirely sympatico, creating a once-heard-never-forgotten theme that is truly ominous, provoking a sense of dread despite, or more likely because of, its minimalist nature.

Surely everybody - general viewers, dedicated cineastes and monster kids alike - can remember their first time watching *Jaws,* and will have a favourite moment, whether it be the initial death of the solo swimmer, the fisherman's head bobbing out of a shipwreck, or Robert Shaw's final fatal slide towards 'Bruce' the shark. Animal attacks would never look better; *Jaws* kickstarted a host of copycats but would remain the pinnacle of the sub-genre.

Jaws 2 (1978) did pretty much what sequels did back then. It escalated everything, throwing in attacks on water skiers and helicopters, and featuring eight deaths overall (as opposed to the original five). It also cost more, - a whopping $30 million - although, in the tradition of diminishing returns, it grossed less than its predecessor. Still, it was hardly a flop, though is less well-considered than *Jaws*, part of which might be due to the cast of

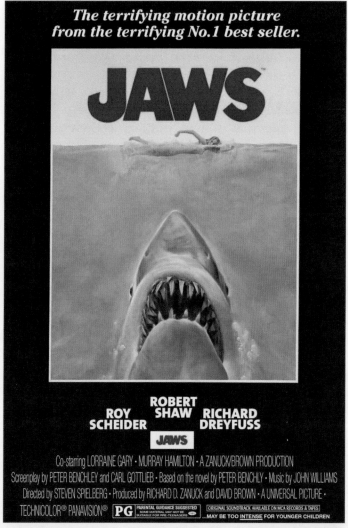

annoying young potential victims, including Keith Gordon of Brian De Palma's *Dressed to Kill* and John Carpenter's *Christine*.

Jaws 2 benefits from filming on the same locations and furthering a strong sense of continuity, featuring the return of Scheider and Hamilton as well as Lorraine Gary as the Chief's wife. Scheider absolutely did not want to return but was legally obliged to make one more film for Universal. Unsurprisingly, Spielberg did not return to direct and the first-choice replacement John D. Hancock was booted after a month. His dark, subtle approach was not what was required and Jeannot Szwarc, who had previously directed the William Castle creature-feature *Bug* (1975) about mutant cockroaches, was brought in. Scheider and Szwarc did not get on, but the movie was completed and proved successful enough to see sequels and a general *Jaws*-inspired crop of marine monstrosities invade cinemas.

These included *Piranha* (1978), Spielberg's personal favourite of the rip-offs. Produced by Roger Corman, this was more than just fun, cheap, disposable B-movie fodder, due to rising names such as director Joe Dante and writer John Sayles. Intended as a tribute to the success of the

original *Jaws*, *Piranha* transcends its original purpose. A horror-comedy blessed with an impressive cast such as Bradford Dillman, Barbara Steele, Kevin McCarthy and Paul Bartel among others, *Piranha* understands its framework and tropes, and isn't shy about showing it. Tension, jeopardy and knowing laughs are piled on in joyful fashion. The plot concerns an alcoholic outdoorsman (Dillman) who teams up with a girl (Heather Menzies) who's been hired to track down missing backpackers. The odd couple explore an old army research plant and discover a shoal of genetically enhanced piranha which escape and make their way downstream towards a kids' summer camp. Gory and funny, with sharp and insightful commentary on the selfishness of big business and lack of moral compasses within the military, the film is as poetic as it is thrilling, gruesome and grimly comic,

benefitting from well shot and edited underwater sequences.

Another well-made effort appeared the previous year, the Dino De Laurentis produced *Orca*, directed by the experienced Michael Anderson. The production boasts a strong cast including Richard Harris, Charlotte Rampling, Robert Carradine, Keenan Wynn, Peter Hooten, Will Sampson and a pre-fame Bo Derek (who loses her leg to the title creature). One of the strengths of *Orca* is that it plays on mysticism to a certain extent and makes much of the killer whale's intelligence and capacity for vengeance.

One of the most memorable scenes is the rather upsetting moment when the Orca's mate is accidentally killed by Harris. When the body is hoisted onboard the fisherman's ship, the whale's unborn foetus squirms free of its wounded body. Horrible stuff, and enough to put the viewer in sympathy with the sea creature. In *Jaws*, Robert Shaw's boat was named the 'Orca', in honour of the one oceanic beast that could best a shark, and Anderson's makes a bold statement immediately by opening with an Orca battering a shark and saving a swimmer's life. A complex movie in many ways, perhaps *Orca* hangs too much on the idea of a whale out for revenge...

but then the *Jaws* series would make the same mistake in the '80s with far worse results.

Less well-crafted *Jaws* cash-ins proliferated too. *Mako: The Jaws of Death* (1976) features Richard Jaeckel as a Vietnam veteran with a psychic link to sharks who decides to gain revenge for them when they are mistreated. Silly stuff, really, but brightened up by the novelty value of a role for Harold Sakata of *Goldfinger* fame.

In 1978, low-budget actor/director/writer/producer Wayne Crawford (yes, he could do it all... sort of) brought *Barracuda* to the screen. A secret government experiment provokes deadly barracuda attacks on the coast of a small. A marine biologist (Crawford) and sheriff (William Kerwin) uncover a plot involving a mentally unstable former war-medic experimenting with fatal consequences.

For all that independent US filmmakers could knock out oddball rip-offs, other countries were also capable.

Tintorera (1977), a UK/Mexico co-production, seemed to be a softcore sex film with added shark carnage. Mexican actors Hugo Stiglitz and Andrés Garcia play shark hunters who spend more time dallying with beautiful ladies than tracking down their target of a menacing tiger shark. Fair play when the ladies in question are portrayed by the likes of Susan George, Priscilla Barnes, Fiona Lewis and Jennifer Ashley, but it makes for a peculiarly unbalanced movie from experienced exploitation director Rene Cardona Jnr.

Also in 1977, Greek director Ovidio G Assonitis assembled a multi-star cast for a monster octopus movie called *Tentacles*. No less than John Huston, Shelley Winters, Henry Fonda, Bo Hopkins, Claude Akins and Cesare Danova were on board, but the film was a mess. For a start, octopi don't have tentacles, they have arms. But pettiness aside, the production had bigger things to worry about, such as when the near-million-dollar prop octopus got lowered into the water… and promptly sank!

In 1978, *Cave of Sharks* directed by Tonino Ricci presented a bizarre melting pot of underwater people, mind-controlled sharks and the Bermuda Triangle. American guest star Arthur Kennedy must have wondered what on earth had happened to his career amidst poor performances and cardboard effects.

Perhaps more could be expected of Italian exploitation director Antonio Margheriti? Sadly not. When Margheriti presented the multi-nation co-production *Killer Fish* in 1979, the killer piranha content was smothered by subplots involving jewel thieves, lost treasure and disaster movie tropes. The good-looking cast of Lee Majors, James Franciscus, Karen Black and Margaux Hemingway didn't save it.

Moving inland, there were a couple of outbreaks of crocodylia, although neither were typical nature fights back tales. Tobe Hooper's *Eaten Alive,* his 1976 follow-up to *The Texas Chainsaw Massacre*, featured more 'backwoods inbred kills unfortunate visitors', but Neville Brand's demented cowboy hotelier did use his pet crocodile to kill tourists and troublemakers (or at least get rid of the evidence). An oft-misunderstood movie, it is deliberately lurid, both colourful and over-the-top in characterisation, with a grim and grisly *Peter Pan* reference running throughout. As one would expect with vintage Hooper, it's an effective shocker: tense, darkly comic and often bloody.

Three years later, Italian exploitation favourites would come together to make *The Great Alligator*. Written by George Eastman, directed by Sergio Martino and starring Barbara Bach, Mel Ferrer and Bobby Rhodes, this beauty sees an African God take the form of a giant man-eating crocodile, attacking tourists at a newly built resort after it becomes angered by encroachment on its land. Filmed in Sri Lanka, it's a sort of alligator *Jurassic Park* with inferior effects but better than many European water monster menaces!

We mustn't forget that despite making 'nature goes wild' pictures very popular, *Jaws* did not invent the genre. There were various nasty critters nipping, nibbling, stinging and squirming in the earlier '70s.

Out of the water, snakes took centre stage for a while. *Stanley* (1972) was directed by William Grefe who would later helm *Mako: The Jaws of Death.* He used the idea of a hero in psychic concord with his deadly pets in both. Here, it is Chris Robinson playing the Vietnam veteran (yes, another) who uses his rattlesnake to put the bite on people he feels have wronged him. This benefited from an atmospheric Everglades setting and hints of Native American folklore and ecological beliefs. Nevertheless, it's a bit silly and it's no surprise that screenwriter Gary Crutcher claimed to have written the entire script in just three whilst high on amphetamines!

1973 saw more unsettlingly weird snake action in *SSSSnake*, a combination of mad doctor and freakshow displays amidst the dusty backroads of America. Strother Martin makes a convincingly

This is Willard
and his friend Ben.
Ben will do anything
for Willard.

This
is the
one
movie
you
should
not see
alone.

GP
ALL AGES ADMITTED
Parental Guidance
Suggested

WILLARD

CINERAMA RELEASING presents WILLARD starring BRUCE DAVISON · SONDRA LOCKE · ELSA LANCHESTER and ERNEST BORGNINE as Martin screenplay by GILBERT A. RALSTON based on the novel "Ratman's Notebooks" by STEPHEN GILBERT music composed and conducted by ALEX NORTH executive producer CHARLES A. PRATT produced by MORT BRISKIN A BCP PRODUCTION a service of Cox Broadcasting Corp. IN COLOR directed by DANIEL MANN FROM C CINERAMA RELEASING

him in the face of a heart condition. None of which stops Ben from forming an army of deadly rodents. Don't you just hate it when that happens? Davison only appears in archive footage during a scene-setting flashback, but it's nice to see a role for Kenneth Tobey, the actor from such classic '50s monster movies such as *The Thing from Another World*, *The Beast from 20,000 Fathoms* and *It Came from Beneath the Sea*.

A less renowned rodent feature appeared that same year, and if I drop the name of director Andy Milligan into the conversation then we all know that we're talking low, low budget! The film has quite a convoluted history though. Originally filmed in England under the title of *The Curse of the Full Moon*, the project's producer William Mishkin asked for more footage. As *Willard* had been such a cinematic hit, Milligan decided to add man-eating rats into the mix, shooting the extra 20 minutes of material back home in Staten Island, New York. Now featuring a glorious combination of lycanthropy, rats and live chickens, the final release title was *The Rats are Coming! The Werewolves are Here!*

For creature feature fans preferring to avoid 'all the fun of the fur', other creepy crawlies were available, such as the previously mentioned *Bug* (1975), about arsonist cockroaches, and based on the Thomas Page novel 'The Hephaestus Plague'. Other movies took their lead from '50s classics such as *Them* and *The Naked Jungle*, offering

misguided scientist and Dirk Benedict (some distance away from his *Battlestar Galactica* and *The A-Team* heroics) is the assistant who is experimented on. The script features both standard snake attacks and something weirder… with Benedict gradually being transformed into a snake-man!

It wasn't all scales and slimy surfaces though. 1972 was also the Hollywood Year of the Rat! And let's face it, the image of veteran movie star Ernest Borgnine being swarmed upon by a multitude of rats has become iconic. Coming from Daniel Mann's adaption of the book 'Ratman's Notebooks' by Stephen Gilbert, *Willard* is a 1971 US horror starring Bruce Davison as a young social misfit called Willard whose only friends are a bunch of rats raised at home, including two that he calls Ben and Socrates. When Willard's boss (Borgnine) kills Socrates, Willard goes on a rampage using his rats to attack and kill. The impressive cast also includes Elsa Lanchester and Sondra Locke, and the film was successful enough to warrant a 1972 sequel called *Ben*, now perhaps most famous for producing the Michael Jackson single of the same name. The plot follows a lonely boy named Danny Garrison who befriends Willard's former pet rat. Ben becomes the boy's best friend, protecting him from bullying and comforting

battling giant ants in the Florida Everglades rarely came up in *Dynasty*!

Empire was released in July 1977 and by December there was an ant invasion TV-movie. *Ants (aka It Happened at Lakewood Manor)* offered standard-sized ants swarming over a holiday resort in their millions! Taking a leaf from so many previous greedy capitalists (see *Jaws, Grizzly, Day of the Animals* and the later *Jaws 2* and *Piranha*), a casino promoter ignores the heroic construction boss played by Robert Foxworth and continues with his plans rather than deal with a poisonous ant infestation. This features a decent cast for a TV production, with Lynda Day George, Bernie Casey, Brian Dennehy, Suzanne Somers and even Myrna Loy helping to gloss over the cliches.

When it comes to nasty little monsters though, surely spiders are top of most people's hate lists. Arachnids had a good eight-legged run during the '70s, with 1975's low-budget *The Giant Spider Invasion* starting us off. Directed by infamous Wisconsin-based exploitation master Bill Rebane, it gets a lot of stick, but is okay. The budget is tiny, but the ambition is huge. The direction might be questionable and yet Rebane understands what he should be doing and occasionally achieves the right results. The cast list includes several notable names, past their lead

ants both big and small.

Empire of the Ants (1977) was directed by long-standing B-movie maestro Bert I. Gordon and was at least nominally based upon an H.G. Wells story. Robert Lansing and British export Joan Collins battle the beasties in a tale that took its lead from the much superior *Them* as the ants featured here were of the giant variety, courtesy of mixed special effects ranging from okay to... really not okay. The performances are decent, and it might well be one of Gordon's better-looking efforts, but it runs too long at 90 minutes. Joan Collins is good value as a con-woman real estate agent, providing good practice for her US soap opera villainess years, although the experience of

actor status (Steve Brodie, Barbara Hale), or B-Movie and television regulars (Leslie Parrish, Alan Hale Jr.) but they have experience and ability. The almost schizophrenic script flipflops consistently between serious giant monster movie and redneck comedy. I saw this at the cinema when I was still junior school age (the UK release had cut out some sexually suspect material to cater for a family audience during the summer holidays) and I didn't notice the car wheels trundling beneath the giant spider model, but I did shiver and shake at the mutilated cattle, and spiders ranging from small to gigantic.

The same year saw *Kiss of the Tarantula*, a tale that has much in common with *Stanley*, *Willard* and *Mako*, focusing on a protagonist who gets revenge on bullies by setting their little pets on them. In this case, a disturbed teenage girl played by Suzanna (then older sister Rebecca) Eddins who deals effectively with

anyone who picks on her mortician father or domesticated spiders.

August 1977 saw William Shatner taking whatever he could get in the quiet years before *Star Trek: The Motion Picture*. He appeared in *Kingdom of the Spiders*, a movie that gets quite a lot of love but is, in fact, very silly indeed. The Shat plays an Arizona vet (no, not a Vietnam vet this time, but an actual veterinarian) who teams up with Tiffany Bolling's arachnologist when the town of Verde Valley is overrun by killer spiders. Director John 'Bud' Cardos also has the great Woody Strode on hand as a doomed local farmer but for all the fast pace of the second half, he can't overcome the speed of spider attacks that cause panicking crowds as people lie covered with cobwebs holding half-eaten burgers - I mean how fast did the spiders spin that web? And how come Shatner survives for ages whilst covered in the critters? As for the farmer's wife who deals with a spider on her finger by shooting her finger off, well it really is *that* silly and is possibly only defended by Shatner lovers. The ending is chilling as the camera reveals the whole town is cocooned in spider webs, but even that seems to steal its ambiguous ending from Hitchcock's infinitely superior *The Birds*.

Airing on television in December 1977, but released to cinemas in Mexico, *Tarantulas: The Deadly Cargo* deals with similar material and has a cast including Claude Akins, Tom Atkins and Pat Hingle. The spiders arrive in crates of coffee beans and are eventually dispatched, believe it or not, through the calming influence of bee sounds!

Talking of which, *The Savage Bees* was a 1976 TV-movie starring Ben Johnson, Michael Parks, James Best and Gretchen Corbett. Like *Tarantulas* and *Ants*, it follows a standard formula but remains easy entertainment as the annual Mardi Gras is disturbed by an influx of African Killer Bees. This

was successful enough to warrant a 1978 sequel, *Terror Out of the Sky*. This time a marching band and a school bus get in the way. Real-life bee wrangler Norman Gary reproduces exactly the same stunts in both. Other bee attacks during the '70s, included Curtis Harrington's TV-movie *Killer Bees* starring Gloria Swanson and Kate Jackson and the preposterous Mexican B-movie *The Bees* that included ill-matched stock footage, obvious dummies used in place of actors and awful dialogue such as "That's adding incest to injury!" However, the ridiculousness of it all makes it a fun watch, bolstered by performances from dependable genre regulars John Saxon and John Carradine.

The one '70s bee film that cannot

be forgiven, of course, is *The Swarm*. Mainly because this is a big-screen blockbuster from disaster movie specialist Irwin Allen, starring a stellar cast of Michael Caine, Richard Widmark, Henry Fonda, Katharine Ross and many more. Ben Johnson appears too, but probably preferred being in *The Savage Bees*. That might have been TV fodder, but it didn't have disastrous direction, editing and dialogue, tied to cheap special effects.

Nightwing (1979) was better - a story of a plague of killer bats terrorising a Native American reservation. Directed by skilled veteran Arthur Hiller and based on Martin Cruz Smith's novel, it is a crazy mix of animal attacks, environmentalism and mysticism, but it's a lot of fun with a strong cast including David Warner, Nick Mancuso, Stephen Macht and Kathryn Harrold.

Not even the cuter creatures made things easier for audiences in the '70s

either. One might be expected to be safe with cats and dogs, but oh no!

Remember René Cardona Jnr, the director of *Tintorera* with that Mexican beefcake Hugo Stiglitz? In 1972 they teamed up to make *Night of 1000 Cats*, about a wealthy playboy who kidnaps young women and then feeds them to his cats. Not really the be-whiskered ones' fault really, but when they develop a routine… This one is quite nasty but also fairly inept.

Another case of 'don't blame the moggies' crops up in *The Uncanny* (1977), the Canadian-financed anthology that Milton Subotsky produced after the end of Amicus Productions. The film retained the structure of many of the Amicus films but here there was a cat theme. Horror legend Peter Cushing plays a writer trying to convince his publisher Ray Milland that the feline world is smart, evil and ready to take over the world. As proof, he offers three stories for consideration. The first, set in London, 1912, shows the cats of a murdered old lady taking a pretty deserved revenge on the deceased's family and staff. Susan Penhaligon is the young lady who feels the sharp end of the claw. Next up is a tale set in Quebec and featuring Chloe Franks, the young actress who appeared in several Amicus movies from a young age. Sadly, she and the other young actress in this story are awful, as is the story itself, a black magic tale that

sees a bullied orphan with a pet cat use her deceased mother's witchcraft to aid a feline-related punishment. Perhaps unwisely, the final segment is a comic one, unbalancing proceedings somewhat, but at least it features ace film villain Donald Pleasence as a 1930s actor who is plagued by a cat after he murders his wife. The film ends with Milland under cat hypnosis burning the only copy of the tales whilst the furballs chase Cushing through the Canadian streets to his death. The problem is that it's hard to make a cat seem menacing when you have to virtually throw it at the actor who is supposed to be under attack.

Likewise with dogs, though David McCallum's career survived playing a University Professor in the 1976 non-epic *Dogs*. Yet another dodgy government experiment could be to blame for messing with canines via pheromones. A pre-*Dallas* Linda Gray has minimal screentime but has been since elevated to second billing on some releases courtesy of her later soap success. As with the feline films, *Dogs* suffers most from the inability to convincingly shoot footage of the animals looking effectively vicious. Yet it didn't stop Albert Band giving the world's must famous vampire his own furry best friend in *Zoltan… Hound of Dracula* (1977) and Curtis Harrington gave television *Devil Dog: Hound of Hell* in 1978. Harrington did seem to love his critters, having

previously come up with *The Cat Creature* (1973) and *Killer Bees* (1974).

Mind you, if making cats and dogs seem scary then take pity on poor William F. Claxton, who had to try and make something menacing out of rabbits with *Night of the Lepus* (1972). Based on a 1964 sci-fi novel 'The Year of the Andy Rabbit' (yes, really), *Lepus* failed dramatically by utilising domestic rabbits filmed against miniatures and stuntmen dressed in fur. No doubt the stars Stuart Whitman, Janet Leigh, DeForest Kelley and Rory Calhoun all sought new agents after this debacle. Ironically, 1978 would see a truly horrific rabbit movie find great success when Martin Rosen wrote, produced and directed *Watership Down*, an animated version of Richard Adams' novel. Despite being intended as a family film about the wonders of nature, it featured some incredibly upsetting violence.

It stands to reason that the bigger animals had more chance of being effectively menacing, and the ursine family were considerably more successful. If you want to more then just bear with me…

In 1970, the Polish folk horror movie *Lokis* told the tale of a 19th century pastor who meets a Lithuanian family that includes a mad matriarch who was once as a young woman attacked by a bear. Locals suspect her son of being a son of a b… well, bear. A death from bite wounds follows but was it man or bear?

Of course, in the wake of *Jaws*, Americans independents were keen to ride the waves and there was no reason why it couldn't be done without water. In 1977, Chuck D. Keen and Brian Russell were cheeky enough to write a screenplay that even ripped off the title and came up with

Claws. Here a grizzly bear exacts revenge on trappers and wages war on the human race, including a logger, campers, hikers, hunters, a boy scout and the local law - altogether now, "I Chomped the Sherriff!" This picture benefited from being set in Alaska and using decent stock footage. However, it had been beaten to release by a superior bear picture - *Grizzly* (1976).

There is no avoiding the fact that it slavishly sticks to the tried and tested *Jaws* formula. Most obviously, a killer beast (big, even for its species) roaming a leisure and tourist attraction just as vacation time begins and the small-town authorities are being stubborn about taking precautions. *Grizzly* offers Christopher George as the forest ranger, Richard Jaeckel as the hunter/expert and Andrew Prine as the Vietnam veteran who provides a helicopter and a bloody big gun. Is it derivative? Of course, but it is also tremendous fun, often tense, sometimes funny and occasionally shocking. The winner here is the location work and tight editing/direction thanks to William Girdler. It looks fantastic and the slightly lower value cast and budget works effectively as the viewer is aware that anything might happen. Somehow *Grizzly* rises above being derivative and offers a solid and exciting hour and a half of action, drama and mild chills. It is a hell of a ride and William Girdler seemed set to progress to

great directorial heights. He went on to direct the similarly themed *Day of the Animals* in 1977, a film that not only recast Richard Jaeckel and Christopher George but also Teddy the bear. Which leads us neatly into the final part of our overview... the 'Monster Mash' wherein more than one type of creature decides to bite back.

Day of the Animals is presented in full-on eco-warrior mode, something that occurs rather a lot in these '70s flicks - one in the eye for climate

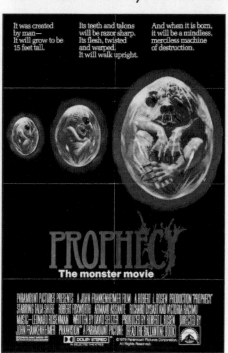

deniers who claim that this sort of concept is so-called 'woke' hysteria of the 21st century. B-movies have been warning us for decades. Here damage to the planet's ozone layer has affected all animals at high altitudes. A group of disparate hikers find themselves under attack from various animals and must make their way to safety, despite ozone layer depletion causing psychosis in them also, particularly Leslie Nielsen, who memorably strips to the waste and attempts to wrestle a grizzly! There are also dogs, birds of prey and snakes, amongst other beasts and whilst the script does at times seem to be a structured presentation of angry animals, each taking their turn in the spotlight, it actually remains quite tense. Girdler knew better than most how to make these things work on a lower budget. Tragically, he died mere years later, whilst flying and looking for new locations for future films. A great loss.

Remember, Bert I. Gordon taking a H.G. Wells short story and creating the not very similar *Empire of the Ants* (1977). Well, he played that trick first the previous year with *Food of the Gods*, but this time it was Marjoe Gortner, Pamela Franklin and Ida Lupino battling oversized chickens, wasps, grubs and overgrown rats! Yet again, it was the ecology fighting back against bad science. This was also the theme of the bewildering, but bloody brilliant *Prophecy* directed by no less a star director than John

Frankenheimer. Starring Robert Foxworth, Talia Shire and Armand Assante, this sees pollution mutating various creatures including salmon, raccoon and tadpoles, but it is a mutated bear that is the real beast of the piece.

It is interesting to note that the ecological warnings lasted throughout the decade of the '70s. *Prophecy* arrived in 1979, but as far back as 1972, cinema audiences were being warned about inappropriate waste disposal. I have saved till last a movie that is far better than it has any right to be, though that might not be agreed upon by all film fans! I refer, of course, to the mighty *Frogs*, the picture that pits such age diverse Hollywood greats as Ray Milland and Sam Elliott against, well not just frogs actually. No, here in the Everglades, the frogs are seen less than toads, but there are also deadly attacks by leeches, snakes, birds, butterflies, spiders and alligators. One must suspend one's disbelief way on high to accept reptiles or amphibians mounting intelligent attacks (in one scene even managing to combine various chemicals to concoct a poison), but the whole hysterical scenario is drenched in hot and humid Southern States atmosphere.

The '80s would bring more of these types of movies: more sharks, more alligators, more cats and dogs... but the '70s was the great decade of the ecological vengeance movie. The best(ial) of them all!

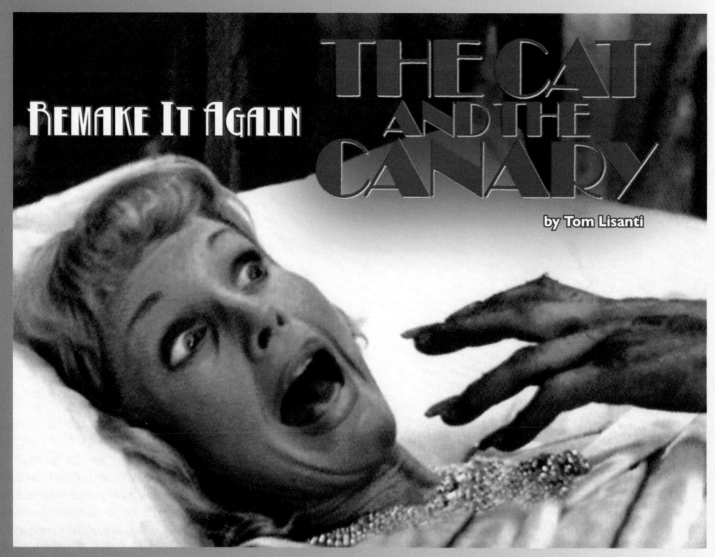

REMAKE IT AGAIN

THE CAT AND THE CANARY

by Tom Lisanti

In late 1974, G.W. Films Limited/EMI Film Distributors produced and released an all-star movie version of Agatha Christie's novel 'Murder on the Orient Express'. Albert Finney starred as Belgian detective Hercule Poirot, investigating the murder of a passenger in the first class section of the famous train as it journeys from Istanbul to London. The list of suspects included such esteemed actors as Lauren Bacall, Ingrid Bergman, Sean Connery, John Gielgud, Wendy Hiller and many more. The film was a critical and box office hit. Soon after, two movies complete with all-star casts went into production to try to capitalize on the success of *Orient Express*. One was *Death on the Nile*, based on another Christie book, with Peter Ustinov taking over from Finney as Poirot. The other was yet another remake of the classic haunted house mystery, *The Cat and the Canary*.

The Cat and the Canary by John Willard began as a one-act play and then was expanded into a full-length stage thriller, premiering on February 7, 1922, at the National Theatre in New York City. It was a straightforward reading-of-the-will mystery with heiress Annabelle West (Florence Eldridge) inheriting a fortune from the deceased Cyrus West. She is the sole heir with the West surname.

However, to collect her fortune, she must survive the night in his creepy mansion to prove she is legally sane. If not, there is a second will with the name of an alternate heir. Accompanying her are the rest of Cyrus' greedy, irate family, including one member who is mentally deranged.

The play was a huge hit and in 1927 a silent film version, directed by Paul Leni, was released by Universal Pictures with Laura La Plante as Annabelle. A talkie retitled *The Cat Creeps* followed in 1930 directed by Rupert Julian with the heroine now played by Helen Twelvetrees. This was produced by Carl Laemmle who also did a Spanish language version that same year called *La Voluntad del Muerto* starring Lupita Tovar. *The Cat and the Canary* came back to the big screen for the fourth time in 1939 as a star vehicle for comedian Bob Hope and lovely Paulette Goddard, with more emphasis on comedy than scares.

Almost thirty-five years had passed before producer Richard Gordon decided to dust off the play and bring it back to the big screen. Explaining why to Alex Gordon for 'Fangoria' magazine in 1978, Gordon said: "The subject offers pure entertainment in the classic movie sense, with all the modern ingredients of action, romance and horror. Paul Leni's silent version had, of necessity, to make certain changes in the story to accentuate the director's expressionist visual style. The immensely popular Bob Hope version was adapted entirely to Hope's comedy style. Our screenplay, written by Radley Metzger, has gone back to the original play. We believe we have more closely preserved the spirit of Willard's play than any of the previous films."

Partnering with Radley Metzger was odd since he was well-known for his artsy, soft-core porn movies. A graduate of City College in New York, he began directing English-dubbed versions of many foreign movies including one German film acquired by Gordon. This is how they met and became friends. By the late '60s, Metzger was directing such sexy hits as *Camille 2000* and *The Lickerish Quartet* before moving into more hardcore features using the name Henry Paris. When asked by author Tom Weaver, for the book 'The Horror Hits of Richard Gordon', how he'd settled on Metzger as his director, Gordon replied: "I used to talk to him often about the possibility that one day we might do something together. When I decided that I would like to make *The Cat and the Canary*, I mentioned it to him and he reacted very enthusiastically, and so we came to the conclusion that this was a good time to do something together, especially as he was interested in writing the screenplay as well as directing."

With a director and screenplay in place, Gordon now had to cast the key roles. Since the movie was going to be filmed in England, the producer wanted a mixture of American and British actors. It seems that Carol Lynley was the first choice to play British fashion designer Annabelle West. Gordon was aware that she had made a fair number of films and TV shows in the UK. He also knew she was popular in England and liked working there.

Carol jumped at the chance to bring her interpretation of Annabelle West to the big screen and said in the Bear Manor Media book 'Carol Lynley: Her Film & TV Career in Thrillers, Fantasy & Suspense' by Tom Lisanti (yes, that's me!): "It was an excellent part and I liked the character a lot. I had done English accents before and I am quite good at it if I do say so. I enjoyed playing British roles especially working with a British cast."

The lone American relative was the character of Paul Jones, a songwriter. This was the role beefed up for Bob Hope in the 1939 version though the character was renamed Wally Campbell. Here he is played by the personable Michael Callan. Unfortunately, the budget did not allow the producers to reach out to a more bankable leading man at the time, but Gordon was satisfied with his choice.

In the play and the previous film version, the lawyer Crosby was played by a man. The producers tried to cast one but hit several snags. The closest to getting the part was James Mason but then he wanted to rewrite the screenplay. Casting director Rose Tobias Shaw then

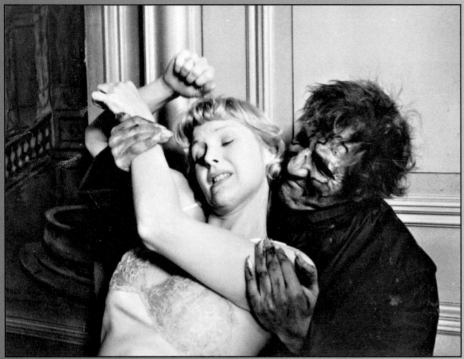

suggested that since they were trying to modernize the story by changing the period from the '20s to the '30s and including a filmed will reading (with Cyrus West badgering his heirs), perhaps Crosby should be played by a woman. Gordon and Metzger liked that idea and her first suggestion, Academy Award winner Wendy Hiller, took the role of Allison Crosby.

The role of Cyrus West was taken by Wilfrid Hyde-White after Robert Morley and Alastair Sim passed on it. Also signed were Honor Blackman as big game hunter Susan Sillsby; Olivia Hussey as her cousin and "roommate" Cicily Young; Edward Fox as Hendricks, a psychologist from the nearby asylum for the criminally deranged; and stage actress Beatrix Lehmann (after Flora Robson, Cathleen Nesbitt, and Elisabeth Bergner all declined) as the housekeeper Mrs. Pleasant.

Causing the biggest casting headache for the production was Horst Buchholz. He was hired to play dashing British pilot Charlie Wilder but dropped out days before production was to commence. British actor Peter McEnery had been cast as surgeon-turned-pharmacist Harry Blythe. Instead, he replaced Buchholz, and Wilder and casting director Rose Shaw brought in Academy Award nominee Daniel Massey to play Blythe.

Filming began in December 1976. The creative team decided that they did not want to shoot on sets in a studio. Associate producer Ray Corbett recommended Pyrford Court in Surrey, outside London. It was the ancestral home of Lord Iveagh of the Guinness Trust, which was founded to help find affordable housing for low-income families. *The Omen* also shot sequences at Pyrford Court. Both exteriors and interiors were shot at this location.

The house was empty, so set decoration was needed and, as might be expected from an unlived English manor, the working conditions were not the greatest. Per Gordon in Tom Weaver's book: "We were shooting in the winter, and it was very cold. Everybody was sort of huddling around space heaters in the library and trying to keep warm in between shooting. [The house] was not properly heated. Of course, the lights from the filming helped to warm it up, but it was not the most comfortable location in the world."

Meanwhile, the cast was not so impressed with their director, Radley Metzger. Carol Lynley revealed: "He didn't do much directing. Only thing he would say is 'Print it.' Considering he had a cast that included Dame Wendy Hiller, Wilfrid Hyde-White and all these well-known and well-respected actors, he didn't do much with us. I was told before we started filming that his background was in softcore porn. I had never met anybody who had worked in that industry on either side of the camera. We had lunch prior and he seemed alright to me."

Lynley added, "One day we were talking about Radley and some of the cast had nicknamed him Rattles. I never called him that. I think it was because he was quiet and a bit nervous. But when you are working with actors of this caliber you don't have to worry about a lot."

Per Gordon, most of the cast behaved as seasoned professionals and went with the flow. Carol Lynley returned the compliment and said Richard Gordon "was delightful and professional. When on the set, he never interfered with anything."

As for how the cast got along, Olivia Hussey remarked: "Carol Lynley was very professional and sweet. I loved talking to Honor Blackman and to Michael Callan - really fun people. Also, Daniel Massey whose sister Anna (I worked with her on stage in *The Prime of Miss Jean Brodie*) sent me much love."

Richard Gordon knew he had assembled an esteemed cast and made sure they were treated with the utmost respect. Carol recalled: "The actors, or artistes as they called us, would have lunch every day around this long table in what they called the artiste's dining room. It was only actors - no crew. Dame Wendy would always sit at the head of the table because the English are very formal with stuff like that. She was a sweetheart. I knew Michael Callan from New York. He's an excellent, excellent actor but got sidetracked by being pleasant and nice. Overall, I was so fascinated and honored to be working with Dame Wendy, Olivia Hussey, Honor Blackman, and the entire cast."

Not all went smoothly though. Daniel Massey and Peter McEnery both behaved badly. Massey did not take it all seriously and was drinking at the time. Carol remarked: "I liked Daniel Massey but he could be grumpy. He was always complaining about Radley. We would stick up for him and say: 'Come on, he's doing a decent job.' Daniel was not happy about working with him and let it be known."

As for Peter McEnery, during the filming of a scene where most of the cast is assembled around the dining room table for supper, Metzger needed a few more minutes to get an important shot. McEnery announced it was lunchtime, got up and walked off the set, shocking the crew and his costars. Most offended, per Richard Gordon, was Wendy Hiller who yelled after him in a bellowing voice: "I think that is one of the most obscene gestures I've ever encountered in my career."

While in production, Gordon ran a full-page ad in 'Variety' touting the movie. It read: "It's 1934 (and appearing in suspiciously alphabetical order) are Honor Blackman, Michael Callan, Edward Fox, Wendy Hiller, Olivia Hussey, Beatrix Lehmann, Carol Lynley, Daniel Massey, Peter McEnery, Wilfrid Hyde-White in *The Cat and the Canary*. Produced by Richard Gordon. Directed by Radley Metzger."

The Cat and the Canary opens in 1904 at Glencliff Manor with a scene of a cat eyeing a caged canary while the voice of a small boy is heard calling for the feline. As the boy runs out of the forest to join a wheelchair-bound old man Cyril West (Hyde-White, who steals the movie) calling out for "Miou Miou", the camera pans to the murdered cat hanging from a tree. Explaining the opening, Richard Gordon revealed: "I felt that we needed something to grab the audience in the beginning because by the nature of the story, once you get underway, there has to be quite a lot of dialogue and exposition before you come to any action. In order to sort of 'reassure' audiences that they were going to see something that would be in nature of a thriller, we wanted an opening sequence that would grab everybody's attention and make them wonder, 'What's all this about?' They would keep that thought in the back of their minds, and eventually it would all tie up together."

The film then jumps to 1934 and the twentieth anniversary of West's death. It is a dark and stormy night. The deceased's attorney Allison Crosby (wonderfully played by Hiller) and trusted housekeeper Mrs. Pleasant (Lehmann) unchain a crate containing Cyrus' will as cars begin to pull up outside the home. In a novel twist from the original, the will is read on film, with synchronized sound, by the deceased. As they remove the reel, they notice a live moth, which raises suspicions, since the crate should have remained sealed since 1914.

The invited West family begin to enter. Harry Blythe (Massey) is a former surgeon who was involved in a scandalous mishap that cost him his license and is now a pharmacist. His nemesis is his cousin Charlie Wilder (McEnery), a WWI flying ace who worked as a stunt man in Hollywood and now endorses toothpaste. Both are bitter rivals for the attention of their lovely, distant cousin Annabelle West. Susan Sillsby (Blackman) is a world-famous big game hunter accompanied by her cousin and "roommate" Cicily Young (Hussey). Jokey Paul Jones (Callan) is an American songwriter. The last guest to arrive is Annabelle (Lynley), an aspiring fashion designer.

After the cousins get reacquainted, Mrs. Crosby calls them to dinner and they are joined by Cyrus West on film. He berates his descendants unmercifully and entertainingly, calling them "leeches", "a bunch of bastards" and "parasites" in the movie's most amusing moments. The dinner served by Mrs. Pleasant is the exact one Cyrus is eating right down to the wine. In one great moment, Mrs. Pleasant walks from right to left behind the screen placed at the head of the table just as she did back in 1914. This was filmed with perfect timing and symmetry. As the potential heirs banter back and forth and make side deals, Cyrus finally reveals that his heir is anyone with the surname of West. A gleeful Annabelle is the sole living West with that name, so she inherits his entire estate including the fabulous West diamond necklace. There is one stipulation. She must spend the night in the manor and if by morning she survives or is not declared insane, the fortune is hers. If not, there is a second film which reveals the next in line for the inheritance.

After the will is read, the guests mingle about the hallways and rooms of the manor. The walls are painted white and it is sparsely furnished except for the library and bedrooms that were reopened for the occasion. Of the few pieces of furniture left, most are covered with white sheets making the house quite bright. Richard Gordon commented in Tom Weaver's book: "That was Radley's concept and I think it worked well. We didn't want it to be yet another 'spooky old country house horror film' where everything takes place in the middle of the night. That was too old-fashioned, I think that idea had sort of rather gone out of style by then."

Dr. Hendricks (Edward Fox) makes a crashing entrance through the window. Claiming nobody heard his knocking, he apologizes, but explains that he runs the insane asylum down the road and that one of their patients has escaped. He is highly dangerous and likes to sneak into houses where he waits until all are asleep and then pounces like a cat with his claw-like fingernails. In one creepy scene, the disfigured hand reaches out to rip off the West necklace from a slumbering Annabelle, who awakens and screams in fright. Her relatives come rushing to her room but find no trace of an intruder and begin questioning Annabelle's sanity. Soon after, people begin disappearing (Crosby and Susan) and are later found murdered. Annabelle is then snatched and dragged to the basement. Of course, the killer is revealed to be a disgruntled family member, aided by a cohort. Annabelle survives the ordeal with help from her American cousin who saves her from being butchered. The movie ends with a beaming Annabelle and Paul in a kiss that makes you wonder why Annabelle seems to like keeping it in the family, so to speak.

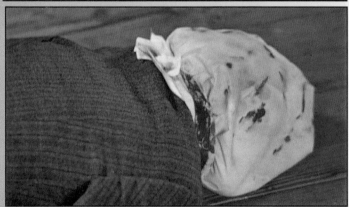

A seasoned distribution deal maker, Richard Gordon had several of them in place. He first wanted *The Cat and the Canary* to open in England, but the distributor

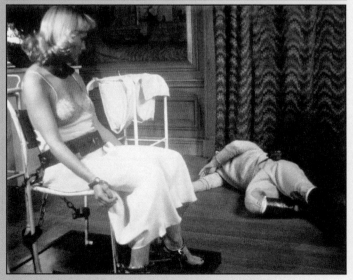

in Italy beat him to the punch. However, the distributor advertised the movie as "Agatha Christie's *The Cat and the Canary*." A letter from her estate threatening a lawsuit quickly brought it to light. Marketing materials supplied by the production company quoting the review in 'Films in Review' that read "infinitely superior to *Death on the Nile*" had confused the distributor into thinking *Cat* was also by Christie, and they blamed it all on Richard Gordon. It is unclear if that really helped the movie in Italy where it was a moderate hit, finishing as the 85th highest grossing movie for the period 1978-79.

The Cat and the Canary was then released in England (via Gala Film Distributors), France, Germany and eventually all over the world except in the United States.

The mystery is equally suspenseful and amusing. It is wonderfully acted, stylishly directed by Radley Metzger,

and keeps the audience guessing. Setting it in a sparsely decorated mansion was a wise decision which adds to the tension. The role of Annabelle West needs to be cast well to make *The Cat and the Canary* successful and Carol Lynley does the part justice, following in the illustrious footsteps of Laura La Plante and Paulette Goddard, among others. She gives an excellent, nuanced performance as Annabelle, complete with a very convincing British accent. Reviews from various countries were fair to good, with Wilfrid Hyde-Whyte and Wendy Hiller receiving the most kudos. Terry Boyce of the 'South China Morning Post' thought the film "attracted a brilliant cast with just about everyone you could wish to have for a tale of mystery and suspense." Liam Lacey of 'The Globe and Mail' unfairly compared it to the superior *Murder on the Orient Express* and called *The Cat and the Canary* "a spoof within a thriller within a star vehicle." As for the cast, he quipped: "Carol Lynley... providing much of the suspense by spending most of the movie in a diaphanous slip and threatening to bare her bosom to fate or temptation." He disliked Michael Callan and remarked that he gave "the only directly offensive performance."

In August 1978, it was reported that Radley Metzger's company Audubon signed a deal with Cinema Shares International (CSI) to release *The Cat and the Canary* in the U.S. When asked why Audubon did not just distribute it in the U.S., Metzger replied: "It wasn't really our kind of film, we couldn't have done it justi... even one as elaborate as that. Richard Gordon sold it in almost every country in the world. Quartet Films had it. They were a substantial art distributor. They had *Breaker Morant*. So, it did well worldwide for us."

CSI had until the end of 1978 to get the movie in theaters. It was accepted and played the Miami Film Festival where the critic in 'Variety' commented that the movie "is plagued by schizophrenia, as though it couldn't decide whether to emulate Neil Simon or William Castle." After praising the comedic turns by Michael Callan and Wilfrid Hyde-Whyte, the review ended stating that it would draw audiences "more interested in style than substance. Metzger's direction is faithful to the genre, and Alex Thompson's photography sports a lushness similar to and evocative of *Murder on the Orient Express* and *Death on the Nile*."

To help with the promotion for its theatrical release, Audubon delivered to CSI "a trailer (produced by the film's London-based producer Richard Gordon), artwork, and assorted promo materials." CSI then submitted the thriller to the New York Film Festival, but it was rejected. Believing that it needed that venue to launch a proper national release, CSI gave up on the film and booked it for one day into the Coral Ridge Theatre in Fort Lauderdale, Florida during the last week of December 1978 in order to meet its contractual obligations. CSI then struck a deal to sell the pay TV rights to Home Box Office. However, Audubon filed a lawsuit in February 1979 blocking that sale and claimed that CSI breached its agreement.

In August 1979, the N.Y. State Supreme Court agreed with Audubon, which won back theatrical, pay TV, and television rights. This case was closely followed because it was "a rare instance of attempting to legally define what constitutes a best-efforts 'theatrical release' as the term is used in standard distribution contracts." Judge Frank J. Blangiardo found in favor of Audubon after a three-day trial due, in part, to the fact that the one-day showing did not include any print promotion, TV and radio spots or trailers. Testimony from defense witnesses from CSI was also used against the company where staff admitted CSI felt the movie had "little theatrical value."

Sadly for the movie and the cast, it was a hollow victory. No other distributors were interested in releasing *The Cat and the Canary*, which may have been considered outdated compared with the popular slasher movies of the time such as *Halloween* and *Friday the 13th*. In 1981 and 1982, it played in a few art houses in the major cities and notices were better than expected. Richard L. Shepard of 'The New York Times' called it a "breezy, pleasant enough diversion" and he found Carol Lynley to be a "lusciously designed heroine." Susan King of the 'Los Angeles Times' remarked that "Carol Lynley and Daniel Massey seem to be having a good time mugging away in this 'dark and stormy night' horror story." While most reviewers loved the Hyde-White scenes best, Scott Cain of the 'Atlanta Constitution' raved: "The best scene involves Carol Lynle and Wendy Hiller. Miss Lynley is babbling merrily and turns her back on Dame Wendy for a few moments. Miss Lynley does not see - but the audience does - a bookcase swing open, a cloaked figure reaches out, grab Dame Wendy and abduct her. That's the last time she's seen - alive, that is."

After popping up here and there in theaters around the country, *The Cat and the Canary* became an in-flight movie and then turned up on cable television. It deserved much better. Finally, in 2014, *The Cat and the Canary* and Radley Metzger received their just due when it played at The Film Society of Lincoln Center as part of a retrospective movie tribute to the director and his career. It is available on DVD and is an underrated gem ripe for rediscovery.

Tratto dal racconto di AGATHA CHRISTIE
Il canarino spesso muore di paura quando il gatto gli cammina intorno perche' non sa' di essere al sicuro nella sua gabbia.

IL GATTO E IL CANARINO

Un film di
RADLEY METZGER
con
HONOR BLACKMAN   MICHAEL CALLAN   EDWARD FOX
WENDY HILLER   OLIVIA HUSSEY   BEATRIX LEHMANN
CAROL LYNLEY   DANIEL MASSEY   PETER McENERY
WILFRID HYDE WHITE   Regia di RADLEY METZGER

PHŒNIX

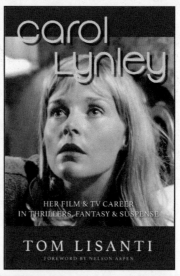

carol Lynley
HER FILM & TV CAREER IN THRILLERS, FANTASY & SUSPENSE
TOM LISANTI
FOREWORD BY NELSON ASPEN

CLOSING CREDITS

Rachel Bellwoar

Rachel is a writer for 'Comicon', 'Diabolique' magazine and 'Flickering Myth'. If she could have any director fim a biopic about her life it would be Aki Kaurismäki.

James Cadman

James first discovered his love of films as a child in the 1980s, happily scanning the shelves of his local video shop. Into his 20s, as part of his media degree, he secured work experience with a major film company which included visiting the set of *Notting Hill* at Shepperton Studios. Now living in Derbyshire with his wife and two young children, James enjoys watching and researching films, especially the '70s work of Eastwood, Friedkin, Peckinpah and Scorsese.

Jonathon Dabell

Jonathon was born in Nottingham in 1976. He is a huge film fan and considers '70s cinema his favourite decade. He has written for 'Cinema Retro' and 'We Belong Dead', and co-authored 'More Than a Psycho: The Complete Films of Anthony Perkins' and 'Ultimate Warrior: The Complete Films of Yul Brynner' with his wife. He lives in Yorkshire with his wife, three kids, three cats and two rabbits!

David Flack

David was born and bred in Cambridge. Relatively new to the writing game, he has had reviews published in 'We Belong Dead' and 'Cinema of the '70s'. He loves watching, talking, reading and writing about film and participating on film forums. The best film he has seen in over 55 years of watching is *Jaws* (1975). The worst is *The Creeping Terror* (1963) or anything by Andy Milligan.

John H. Foote

John is a critic/film historian with thirty years experience. He has been a film critic on TV, radio, print criticism, newspaper and the web, for various sites including his own, Footeandfriendsonfilm.com. He spent ten years as Director of the Toronto Film School, where he taught Film History, and has written two books. The first was an exploration of the films directed by Clint Eastwood, the second a massive volume of the works of Steven Spielberg. Scorsese is next. John has interviewed everyone in film, except Jack Nicholson he quips. His obsession with film began at age 13.

John Harrison

John is a Melbourne, Australia-based freelance writer and film historian who has written for numerous genre publications, including 'Fatal Visions', 'Cult Movies', 'Is It Uncut?', 'Monster!' and 'Weng's Chop'. Harrison is also the author of the Headpress book 'Hip Pocket Sleaze: The Lurid World of Vintage Adult Paperbacks', has recorded audio commentaries for Kino Lorber, and composed the booklet essays for the Australian Blu-ray releases of *Thirst*, *Dead Kids* and *The Survivor*. 'Wildcat!', Harrison's book on the film and television career of former child evangelist Marjoe Gortner, was published by Bear Manor in 2020.

Bryan C. Kuriawa

Based in New Jersey, Bryan has spent many years diving into the world of movies. Introduced to the Three Stooges by his grandfather and Japanese cinema when he was eight, he's wandered on his own path, ignoring popular opinions. Willing to discuss and defend everything from Jesus Franco's surreal outings to the 007 masterpiece *Moonraker*, nothing is off-limits. Some of his favorite filmmakers include Ishiro Honda, Jacques Tati, Lewis Gilbert, Jesus Franco and Jun Fukuda.

James Lecky

James is an actor, writer and occasional stand-up comedian who has had a lifelong obsession with cinema, beginning with his first visit to the Palace Cinema in Derry, (now long since gone) to see *Chitty Chitty Bang Bang* when he was six. Since then, he has happily wallowed in cinema of all kinds but has a particular fondness for Hammer movies, spaghetti westerns, Euro-crime and samurai films.

Tom Lisanti

Tom is an award-winning author specializing in writing about 1960s/1970s Hollywood. His most recent book (#10) is 'Carol Lynley: Her Film & TV Career in Thrillers, Fantasy & Suspense' from BearManor Media. He also has written recent magazine articles for 'Films of the Golden Age' and 'Cinema Retro'. His newest books due in 2023 are 'Dueling Harlows: Race to the Silver Screen Expanded Ed.' and 'Ryan's Hope: An Oral History of Daytime's Ground-Breaking Soap' from Kensington Books. Tom posts regularly on Facebook, Twitter, and his website, sixtiescinema.com. He resides in New York.

Stephen Mosley
Stephen is an actor and writer, whose books include 'Christopher Lee: The Loneliness of Evil' (Midnight Marquee Press), 'Klawseye: The Imagination Snatcher of Phantom Island', 'The Lives & Deaths of Morbius Mozella', 'TOWN' and 'The Boy Who Loved Simone Simon'. His film articles have appeared in such magazines as 'Midnight Marquee', 'We Belong Dead' and 'The Dark Side'. His film credits include the evil Ear Goblin in *Kenneth*; the eponymous paranormal investigator of *Kestrel Investigates*; the shady farmer, James, in *Contradiction*; and a blink-and-you'll-miss-it appearance opposite Sam Neill in *Peaky Blinders*. Stephen is one half of the music duo Collinson Twin and lives in a dungeon near Leeds.

Brian J. Robb
Brian is the 'New York Times' and 'Sunday Times' bestselling biographer of Leonardo Di Caprio, Keanu Reeves, Johnny Depp and Brad Pitt. He has also written books on silent cinema, the films of Philip K. Dick, horror director Wes Craven, classic comedy team Laurel and Hardy, the *Star Wars* movies, Superheroes, Gangsters, Walt Disney and the science fiction television series *Doctor Who* and *Star Trek*. His illustrated books include a History of Steampunk and an award-winning guide to J.R.R. Tolkien's Middle-earth. A former magazine and newspaper editor, he was co-founder of the Sci-Fi bulletin website and lives near Edinburgh.

Allen Rubinstein
Allen grew up in an upper-middle-class neighborhood in suburban Connecticut. He writes about movies and history and tries to reveal the truth wherever possible. He works with his wife on a teaching organization called The Poetry Salon (www.thepoetrysalon.com) in Costa Rica while taking care of far too many cats. He has not yet told his parents that he's an anarcho-syndicalist.

Peter Sawford
Peter was born in Essex in 1964 so considers himself a child of the '70s. A self-confessed film buff, he loves watching, reading about and talking about cinema. A frustrated writer his whole life, he's only recently started submitting what he writes to magazines. His favourite director is Alfred Hitchcock with Billy Wilder running him a close second. He still lives in Essex with his wife and works as an IT trainer and when not watching films he's normally panicking over who West Ham are playing next.

Aaron Stielstra
Aaron was born in Ann Arbor, Michigan and grew up in Tucson, AZ. and NYC. He is an actor, writer, illustrator, soundtrack composer and director. After moving to Italy in 2012, he has appeared in 4 spaghetti westerns and numerous horror-thrillers - all of them unnecessarily wet. He recently directed the punk rock comedy *Excretion: the Shocking True Story of the Football Moms*. His favorite '70s actor is Joe Spinell.

Ian Taylor
Ian dabbled in horror fiction in the early '90s before writing and editing music fanzines. He later adjudicated plays for the Greater Manchester Drama Federation but enjoys film analysis most. Over the last five years, he has become a regular writer and editorial team member for 'We Belong Dead' magazine and contributed to all their book releases. This has led to writing for Dez Skinn's 'Halls of Horror', Allan Bryce's 'Dark Side' and Hemlock's 'Fantastic Fifties', amongst others. His first solo book 'All Sorts of Things Might Happen: The Films of Jenny Agutter' was recently released as a 'We Belong Dead' publication.

Dr Andrew C. Webber
Dr. W. has been a Film, Media and English teacher and examiner for over 35 years and his passion for the cinema remains undiminished all these years later. As far as he is concerned, a platform is where you wait for the 08.16 to Victoria; dropping is something that louts do with litter; and streaming is how you might feel if you were in *Night of the Hunter* being hotly pursued by Robert Mitchum with "Hate" tattooed on his knuckles and Stanley Cortez doing the cinematography.

Steven West
Steven's first published work was as a floppy haired teenager, voice breaking as he scribbled about Terence Fisher for an early issue of 'We Belong Dead' - a useful break from the lingerie section of the Freeman's catalogue. He still writes for the magazine and its spin offs while regularly contributing to 'The Fantastic Fifties' magazine and the UK Frightfest website, alongside www.horrorscreamsvideovault.co.uk. In 2019, Auteur Publishing released his 'Devil's Advocate' book about Wes Craven's *Scream*. Steven lives in Norfolk with his partner, daughter and - thanks to permanent home working - a dozen sock-puppet 'friends'.

Printed in Great Britain
by Amazon